CARNIVORE COOKING FOR COOL DUDES

The incredible new nose-to-tail eating strategy to lose excess body fat, improve performance, speed recovery, and heal inflammation and autoimmunity

BRAD KEARNS
BRIAN McANDREW
WILLIAM SHEWFELT

Carnivore Cooking for Cool Dudes

The incredible new nose-to-tail eating strategy to lose excess body fat, improve performance, speed recovery, and heal inflammation and autoimmunity

Library of Congress Control Number: 2019914852

Paperback ISBN: 978-1-7326745-5-4 eBook ISBN: 978-1-7326745-7-8

Publisher: Bradventures LLC

Please contact the publisher at bradventuresLLC@gmail.com with any questions, concerns, feedback, and to obtain quantity discounts.

Editor: N/A (first draft was perfect)

Proofreading and Indexing: Tim Tate (indexing@warwick.net)

Art Director and Book Design: Caroline De Vita (carolinedevita.com)

Cover photo: Janée Meadows

Dudes cooking photos: Natalie Brenner (NatalieBrennerPhoto.com)

Recipe photos and testing: Sarah Steffens (savorandfancy.com)

Recipe photos on pages 72, 81, 117, 130, 133, 160, 222, 229, 231: Dolores Lusitana (situationbook.com)

Spot illustrations: Caroline De Vita

Fabulous kitchen hostess at her fabulous kitchen: Devyn Sisson

Other photos: Steven "eWildlife Photo" Kobrine, Brian McAndrew, Grace McAndrew, Brad Kearns, William Shewfelt, Chelsea Bandini, Alan Hurt Jr., Gregory Pappas, Josh Willink, Tatiana, Rawpixel, Robert Acurin, Veeterzy

Printed in the U.S.A.

MAD PROPS FOR THE CARNIVORE DIET FROM FAMOUS PEOPLE

"The nose-to-tail carnivore strategy enables you to enjoy maximum nutrient density in your diet, with minimal exposure to plant antigens that can cause serious problems for sensitive people. In my psychiatry and functional medicine practice, I have seen many examples of remarkable spontaneous healing from chronic autoimmune and inflammatory conditions prompted by a carnivore eating strategy."

— DR. PAUL SALADINO,
psychiatrist and functional medicine physician, author of *The Carnivore Code*

"The idea of a carnivore diet is gaining more credibility every day, especially for sufferers of chronic autoimmune or inflammatory conditions. In my promotion of the Primal Blueprint lifestyle, I have prided myself on maintaining an open mind and being willing to revise my position when new information comes to light. The carnivore premise is extremely compelling and worth investigating further for all ancestral health enthusiasts."

— MARK SISSON,
Primal Kitchen kingpin

"I have been following a carnivore-style diet for nearly two decades in my quest for peak performance in bodybuilding and power lifting. If you want to get lean quickly, and boost your recovery with superior nutrition, carnivore is a proven effective strategy. Naysayers can say what they want, but a six-pack doesn't lie. Try carnivore if you are interested in a body composition breakthrough and a more nutritious diet."

— CHRIS BELL,
bodybuilding legend and inventor of the amazing Sling Shot training aid (markbellslingshot.com)

Our ancestors most certainly were omnivores, but they likely ate plants mostly as a strategy against unsuccessful hunting. If our ancestors were able to bring down a prehistoric wooly mammoth, that estimated three million calories would have fed the band lavishly for months!

— DR. SHAWN BAKER,
orthopedic surgeon, carnivore expert, co-host of *Performance Outliers* podcast, world-record indoor rower at age 51

INTRODUCTION

KEEP READING.
YOU TOO CAN BECOME A
CELEBRATED OBJECT OF DESIRE
BY EATING CARNIVORE!

WELCOME TO YOUR NEW NOSE-TO-TAIL LIFE!

Hey dude, how's it going? Welcome to the exciting world of the carnivore diet. The premise of the carnivore diet is simple: You consume predominantly (or entirely) animal foods with a "nose-to-tail" strategy. You strive for maximum variety (especially with nutrient powerhouses like organ meats) and the highest-quality choices in each food category (grass-fed beef, pasture-raised eggs, wild-caught fish, etc.) to maximize nutritional benefits.

The novel concept of eating exclusively animal foods has taken the ancestral health world by storm because enthusiasts are achieving an assortment of truly amazing results. Chief among them is a reliable and rapid reduction of excess body fat when going carnivore for even just 30 days. Those suffering from chronic autoimmune or inflammatory conditions discover immediate improvement in symptoms that largely resist mainstream medical intervention. Others report improved athletic performance and recovery, particularly a reduction in post-exercise stiffness and inflammation after switching to carnivore.

Don't be influenced by naysayers trashing carnivore as a Burger King binge. The evolved carnivore approach is far from the Standard American Diet pattern of eating objectionable CAFO products (Concentrated Animal Feeding Operations, featuring hormones, pesticides, antibiotics, and environmentally objectionable practices) and focusing almost entirely on muscle meats—which have an inferior nutritional profile to organ meats. Instead, you'll indulge in exotic, colorful, and incredibly nutritious foods: the intense orange hues

of pastured eggs and salmon roe, teeming with important vitamins and minerals; the rich burgundy of liver (perhaps the most nutrient-dense food on the planet) and other organ meats; steaming mugs of bone broth (a great source of hard-to-find agents like collagen and glycosaminoglycans that boost connective tissue health); the omega-3 powerhouses in the oily, cold-water fish SMASH hits family (Sardines, Mackerel, Anchovies, Salmon, Herring), and much more. It's an adventure deep into the foods that nourished human evolution for 2.5 million years.

The most striking (and controversial) aspect of carnivore is the elimination or minimization of the colorful plant foods that have been universally embraced as the foundation of a nutritious diet. Crazy as it sounds, the idea here is that many of us may be mildly or significantly reactive to the *anti-nutrients/antigens/plant toxins* contained in plant foods, even super healthy stuff like leafy greens and cruciferous veggies. It's well known that plants release defensive compounds such as *lectins* (gluten is an example of a lectin) and *phytates* to ward off garden pests, and that these agents can trigger an inflammatory and/or autoimmune response in sensitive individuals. It is for this reason that we take elaborate steps to soak, sprout, or cook assorted plant foods to neutralize plant toxins and render them edible. Plant antigens might also be blamed for the gas, bloating, and other digestive distress you might experience when chugging down a smoothie with a high volume of raw kale, spinach, celery, and ginger.

What makes things difficult is that your sensitivity to plants can often be sub-clinical, stimulating low-grade inflammation or compromising the integrity of your gut lining without any debilitating symptoms. Beyond the familiar examples of extreme reactivity in those with peanut allergies or celiac disease, many of us may unknowingly suffer from sub-clinical conditions to the extent that we have come to view gas, bloating, and transient abdominal pain as normal, and certainly not unhealthy. Consider this recent quip from an elite level athlete friend of ours: "Of course you get bloated from green smoothies, but it's worth it for all that nutrition." Well, an experience with carnivore will get you thinking differently about what's normal, necessary, and healthy. Fasting until noon and then enjoying a powerhouse lunch of liver, egg yolks, and grass-fed beef might just beat a super duper morning green concoction that causes your stomach to pop out for a few hours.

Beyond the direct impact of plant ingestion on digestive function, there are numerous other conditions potentially driven by reactivity that land in the autoimmune or inflammatory categories. The term *autoimmunity* describes an undesirable response by your immune system such that your body is attacking itself. For example, a leaky gut allows undigested foreign particles that have a molecular resemblance to pathogens to enter the bloodstream. In response, your immune system becomes confused and attacks healthy cells—an autoimmune response. Many experts believe this is the root cause of diseases like rheumatoid arthritis, lupus, Hashimoto's, and even multiple sclerosis.

When we talk about inflammation/inflammatory conditions in a negative context, we are really describing *chronic* inflammatory conditions as opposed to the natural and desirable acute inflammatory response. When your muscles get pumped to lift heavy weights or your foot swells from a bee sting, these are desirable types of inflammation that support peak performance or healing. When you dose yourself with gluten every day for decades and go through life with allergies, asthma, dermatitis, psoriasis, acne, acid reflux, headaches, muscle and joint pain, or reproductive problems like polycystic ovarian syndrome, this is chronic inflammation breaking you down and slowly destroying your health and vibrancy. Over the years, your seasonal allergies, swollen ankles in the morning, sore back in the evening, skin rashes, or assorted other conditions that we typically treat with long-term prescription medication can easily get integrated into your perception of "normal."

It's a disturbing prospect to think about spending decades faithfully emphasizing so-called superfoods like kale, broccoli, onions, walnuts, hummus, and almond butter, and then be faced with the prospect that they not only aren't superfoods, but they might even be unknowingly compromising your health. Alas, this has been the case for many sufferers of chronic inflammatory and autoimmune conditions. Carnivore's popularity has exploded in part due to some remarkable healing stories. Embarking on an exclusionary diet consisting almost entirely of animal-sourced foods is designed to give your system a break from plant antigens, with the expectation that you can calm or even eventually eliminate the inflammatory and autoimmune conditions that have been with you for decades.

Leading carnivore promoter Dr. Paul Saladino is a psychiatrist and functional medicine physician who has had outstanding results treating anxiety, depression, and assorted other mental health conditions with a carnivore dietary intervention. Carnivore enthusiast Amber O'Hearn claims to have successfully alleviated her diagnosis of bipolar disorder with a carnivore diet. Mikhaila Peterson, daughter of Dr. Jordan Peterson (Canadian psychologist, author of *12 Rules For Life*, and modern philosopher/thought leader), experienced near-miracle healing from extreme lifelong autoimmune, chronic fatigue and depressive disorders with the carnivore diet. She went from autoimmunity so severe that it resulted in hip and ankle replacements in her teens and twenties, to vibrant health in a short time. Check out meatheals.com for tons of stunning success stories and intriguing commentary.

If you're not suffering from a chronic health condition, the idea of cutting veggies, fruits, nuts, seeds, and of course grains might not entice you as powerfully as someone desperate to heal from mysterious and frustrating illnesses. In which case, you may be more interested in the many other inherent benefits of the carnivore diet, such as the efficient reduction of excess body fat and improved physical and cognitive performance. When you implement a carnivore-style diet, every item on your plate will be nutrient-dense and highly satiating. There are no empty calories in the animal foods category, and the many high-protein offerings provide maximum satiety. Combined with the extremely minimal carb content, you will enjoy stable mood, appetite, and energy levels, instead of the energy roller coaster caused by a high-carbohydrate diet.

Carnivore allows you to efficiently drop excess body fat while eating incredibly satisfying meals, fasting whenever you like, and maintaining high energy levels. You become a fat-burning beast, in the spirit of your primal ancestors who followed a carnivore-friendly diet for the past 2.5 million years. Furthermore, with a tightly focused eating strategy, you eliminate the decision fatigue and depletion of will power that can occur when there is more choice and flexibility in your diet.

While evolutionary biology confirms that humans evolved as omnivores, Dr. Saladino makes a compelling case on his *Get Over Yourself* podcast interview with Brad that plants are merely "survival foods": They have a generally inferior nutritional value to animal foods and were perhaps only consumed as a strategy against unsuccessful hunting. Carnivore leader Dr. Shawn Baker offered a memorable podcast comment that if a primal hunter-gatherer band—typical size of 30 individuals—were able to bring down a prehistoric wooly mammoth, they could feast on an estimated three million calories for months without having to gather anything.

Regarding the predictable objection of missing out on the high antioxidant and micronutrient values in colorful plants, Dr. Saladino and other carnivore advocates point out that plants generate antioxidant benefits because they are *hormetic stressors*—our bodies generate an antioxidant response to address the ingestion of a plant antigen. The benefits of antioxidants are potentially negated by our powerful internal antioxidant production mechanisms. For example, when you are fasting or introducing other hormetic stressors like cold or heat exposure, you up-regulate the internal production of the super-antioxidant *glutathione* and also boost the natural internal cellular detoxification process known as *autophagy*. The essential argument here is that you simply don't need plants to optimize antioxidant and immune function, especially when you can engage in other forms of hormetic stressors like sprint workouts and cold plunges.

The carnivore diet that was once considered a joke for bodybuilder freaks to get cut up for contests is rapidly gaining scientific legitimacy and stunning success stories. Clearly, when you source sustainably raised nose-to-tail animal foods, pastured eggs, wild-caught salmon, and the like, you are enjoying an incredibly nutrient-dense, high-satiety diet, with little or no allergenic or reactivity concerns in the animal foods category. Considering a radical new dietary strategy that challenges your carefully honed and rigid belief system can be a valuable exercise in open-mindedness and critical thinking. It seems that many thought leaders and progressive health enthusiasts like to continually test, evaluate, refine, and re-test a lifestyle strategy. Carnivore may be worth investigating further, especially if you suffer from any frustrating autoimmune or inflammatory conditions.

...you simply don't *need* plants to optimize antioxidant and immune function...

THE "EVOLUTION" OF THE CARNIVORE DIET

Over the time period between 2017-2019, the carnivore diet appeared out of nowhere and became a force to reckon with in the burgeoning ancestral health scene. Well, not "nowhere," as carnivore was clearly a refinement of the broader primal/paleo/ancestral diet that has been going strong for over a decade. The initial arrival of carnivore was met with shock and knee-jerk negativity, but people quickly sat up and took notice of the compelling success stories and scientific rationale for a diet of predominantly or entirely nose-to-tail animal foods.

The resistance that even progressive health enthusiasts might have toward carnivore is reminiscent of how the ancestral approach emerged to challenge conventional wisdom's grain-based, high-carbohydrate, high-insulin-producing Standard American Diet (SAD). The ancestral approach has absorbed plenty of criticism along the way, and it has taken millions of user success stories and mounting scientific studies to convince people that ancestral eating is actually healthy instead of crazy. After all, we like to hold on tight to rigid beliefs and ingrained habits, and the ancestral message is a radical departure from our lifelong programming based on the flawed and dated ideals of the USDA Food Pyramid. Furthermore, the trillion-dollar food, health care, and pharmaceutical industries are heavily vested in the status quo of carb addiction, prescription drug intervention, and disease management instead of wellness lifestyles.

Fortunately, the compelling evidence of 2.5 million years of human evolution as hunter-gatherers, coupled with mounting scientific research, has enabled ancestral eating and lifestyle practices to gain widespread acceptance. We humans have evolved to eat meat, fish, fowl, eggs, vegetables, fruits, nuts and seeds, and acceptable nutrient-dense modern foods such as high-fat dairy products, and high-cacao percentage dark chocolate. From this healthy foundation of ancestral-style eating emerged the ketogenic diet. Again, this is not some wild new gimmick, but an evolution-tested method of manufacturing a clean burning alternative energy source to glucose. Furthermore, the ketogenic diet has been used for over a century as a treatment protocol for drug-resistant seizures because it increases oxygen delivery and blood circulation and reduces inflammation in the brain. Ketones are manufactured in the liver as a by-product of fat metabolism when you are fasting or greatly restricting dietary carbohydrates. They burn more cleanly and efficiently than glucose, giving you a boost in cognitive function, immune function, anti-inflammatory benefits, and rapid removal of excess body fat.

The main purpose and benefit of low-carb eating in general is to help you escape carbohydrate dependency and build what Cool Dudes call *metabolic flexibility*. Metabolic flexibility means you are expert at burning stored body fat, that your liver can make ketones to fuel your brain when you are fasting or significantly restricting carbs, and that you can skip meals comfortably without experiencing a decline in cognitive or physical function. Instead of being highly reliant upon regular feedings of high-carbohydrate meals to function, you reawaken your genetically hard-wired ability to be a fat-burning beast.

Carnivore is distinct from keto because you don't eat plant foods and you don't have to count macros, but it has many similarities. Because you are choosing mostly or all animal foods, you will be consuming an extremely minimal amount of carbohydrates and likely be spending a lot of time in ketosis. On the other hand, the high-protein nature of many of your meals might compromise ketone production at times, because protein consumption stimulates insulin, and insulin shuts off ketosis. Know that protein consumption also stimulates insulin's counterregulatory hormone glucagon, so you don't get an insulin crash from a high-protein meal as you would from a high-carbohydrate meal. In essence, a carnivore approach will afford you most all of the benefits of keto unless you are fighting a specific health condition that entails carefully limiting protein and keeping blood ketone levels high at all times.

Why Carnivore, Dude?

The reason sorry-ass SAD eaters should switch to carnivore is that it will likely save their lives. The grain-based, high-carbohydrate, nutrient-deficient modern diet puts you on an express train to pain, suffering, and accelerated demise. *Hint*: If you stand at attention in the shower, look down, and cannot see your male reproductive organ or your toes, you are riding this express train.

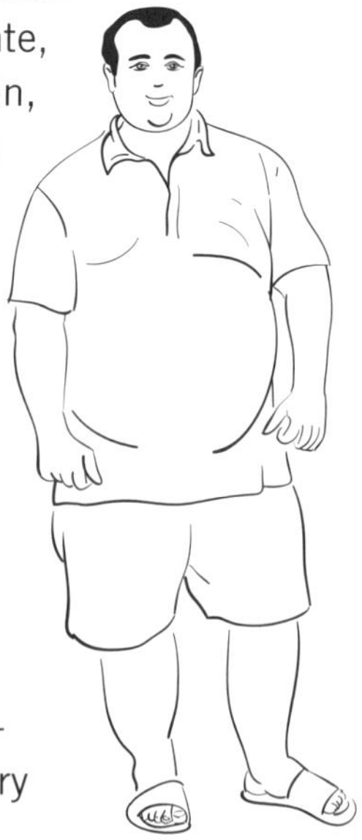

The catch-all term Metabolic Syndrome conveys a checklist of disease risk factors that have reached epidemic proportions in the developed world. A spare tire and hidden jewels suggest your body is in a state of chronic inflammation, chronically excessive insulin production, testosterone suppression, and elevated risk of diabetes, heart disease, cancer, and being banned from Cool Dude group events. Seriously, the shower exam is Dr. Ron Sinha's (Cool Dude author *of The South Asian Diet*) medically validated screening to determine if you have unsatisfactory body composition and related metabolic health risks.

If you are already healthy, fit, and committed to eating natural, nutritious foods, going carnivore or carnivore-ish—at least for a short-duration experiment and possibly as a long-term dietary foundation—can deliver some extremely pleasant surprises relating to improved metabolic and immune function and a possible breakthrough to a superior level of body composition. Here are some of the major reasons for and benefits of eating carnivore:

1. **Desperate Attempt to Heal:** If you are suffering from a medium-to-severe chronic health condition that has resisted mainstream medical treatment protocols, you owe it to yourself to conduct a 30-day strict carnivore experiment for a possible quick and dramatic improvement in your symptoms. You have nothing to lose and lots to gain, so go for it!

2. **Improvement in Sub-clinical Inflammatory or Autoimmune Conditions:** Many carnivore enthusiasts report a significant improvement in digestion and elimination, specifically a near-complete resolution of routine minor bouts of gas, bloating, intestinal pain, and irregular bowel function that most of us seem to accept as an ordinary part of life. Beyond experiencing seamless digestion for the first time ever, many who switch to carnivore report an assortment of surprising health awakenings, where nagging ailments seemingly unrelated to diet improve quickly. These can include anything rooted in inflammation, autoimmunity, or leaky gut syndrome, such as: allergies, asthma, joint pain, assorted mild to serious skin conditions (acne, rosacea, psoriasis, etc.), mood disturbances (depression, anxiety, ADHD, brain fog, etc.), insomnia, sleep apnea, and assorted conditions ending with *"-itis."* Health improvements in these areas are likely the result of giving your system a break from the inflammatory and immune-disturbing effects of plant antigens. Furthermore, a carnivore approach rich in joint compounds from bone broth and bone-in cuts of meat is believed to have gut healing properties. This highly touted "seal and heal" effect on the gut lining of carnivore can address the upstream cause of many chronic health conditions.

3. **Fat reduction:** Carnivore sets you up for weight loss success like no other diet. It's incredibly nutrient-dense and satiating, eliminating the deprivation and struggle often associated with calorie-restriction and carb-restriction diets. Perhaps most beneficial for fat loss is how the narrowing of options with carnivore eliminates the decision fatigue and the depletion of will power that can cause you to backslide and binge your way out of a strict keto plan or a low-fat, plant-based plan. For example, witness how many paleo and keto-approved "substitute" meals and treats there are. You can spend all year indulging in keto brownies and paleo oatmeal to the extent that you never achieve the caloric deficits necessary for fat

loss. And there are plenty of vegan-friendly but insulin-stimulating meals and snacks to keep you stuck despite careful attention to portion control and clean food choices. Carnivore is different. You can only eat so much steak, liver, and pastured eggs until you feel totally nourished and satisfied, and you won't have to deal with an insulin surge or appetite hormone spike in the hours after carnivore meals. Carnivore may be the safest, most pleasurable, most nourishing, most surefire fat-reduction diet you will ever try!

4. Improved Nutrient Density: When you do carnivore the right way, the true superfoods of organ meats, SMASH fish, pastured eggs, and bone broth become dietary centerpieces instead of occasional offerings. When you provide the deep nourishment that your cells and energy systems crave at the genetic level, you experience a magnificent awakening of energy and vitality—even if you already eat a clean, whole food, ancestral-inspired diet.

HOW TO GET STARTED WITH CARNIVORE

A carnivore or even carnivore-ish eating pattern often represents a radical departure from your existing diet, especially if you have been following a grain-based, high-carbohydrate diet for an extended period of time. To maximize nutritional benefits and minimize your chances of backsliding and burnout, you'll want to implement a thoughtful and strategic approach as follows:

1. Clean Up Your Act: Eliminate refined grains (wheat, rice, corn, pasta, cereal) sweetened beverages, sugary snacks and treats, and industrial seed oils (canola, corn, soybean, sunflower, etc.) from your diet so you have a fighting chance of success. If you currently have a fair amount of processed foods, fast foods, and junk foods in the mix, spend three weeks cleaning up your act and bringing in more wholesome, minimally processed foods. Don't worry about initiating a carnivore experiment until you do the work to eliminate dietary toxins, minimize insulin production, and start upregulating your fat burning genes.

2. Choose the Best Foods: Commit to sourcing the highest quality, most sustainable animal products you can find. If your local offerings are limited, utilize Internet resources to get wild-caught fish and grass-fed beef shipped to your door. Some might criticize eating sustainably raised animals and fish as cost prohibitive, but numerous analyses from real consumers actually suggest otherwise. When you eliminate high-insulin stimulating foods and stabilize your appetite hormones, you end up eating fewer meals, fewer snacks and treats, and fewer total calories. Notably, eliminating pricey sweetened beverages, designer energy snacks, and frequent takeout meals generates a huge reduction in your monthly food expenditures that can be reprioritized to choosing higher quality eggs, fish, and beef.

3. Emphasize Nose-to-Tail: Some carnivore enthusiasts report excellent results from merely slamming burgers and steaks. As with an enthusiastic whole foods plant-based eater, the major benefits of restrictive diets are often *what you don't eat*, rather than any special magic of burgers or kale 'n brown rice bowls. To enjoy maximum and lasting benefits of carnivore, make your best effort to consume as many different foods as possible and cover the entire animal in the spirit of our ancestors. Indeed, from the ancient Aztecs to the ancient Greeks to modern day hunter-gatherers, organ meats have been the most prized bounty of the hunt. Like the lion and other apex predators, ancient hunters across the globe were known to feast on warm liver on the spot after a kill. Speaking of budget, the ultimate superfoods of organ meats are incredibly affordable because consumer demand is still minimal. Become a thought leader and culture shaper by increasing your consumption of organ meats!

4. Limit Your Eating Window: It's reported that four out of five Americans eat in a time window greater than 12 hours every day. Since maximum metabolic, hormonal, and immune benefits come when you are in a fasted state, and your digestive function desperately requires down time (especially to facilitate good sleep), strictly observe a maximum eating window of 12 hours per day. For example, if you initiate digestive function at 7 a.m., finish by 7 p.m. Strive to continually progress to eating in an eight-hour time window or even a six-hour time window frequently, as this will hone metabolic flexibility and increase your discipline, focus, and appreciation for healthy meals. *Note*: Even a non-caloric coffee or herbal tea in the morning starts your digestive clock for the day, so take that into consideration with your 12-hour calculation.

5. Pay Attention to Supplementation: Be certain that you are getting adequate sodium, minerals, and electrolytes, because deficiencies in these areas can manifest into general malaise that you might erroneously associate with carnivore eating. If you are a little lax about your consumption of organ meats, bone broth, and high-omega-3 fish, consider some of the supplement recommendations in Tip #6 on page 27 and in Supplement Recommendations for a Carnivore Diet on page 43.

CLIMBING A NEW PYRAMID

You are likely familiar with the USDA Food Guide Pyramid and the many iterations that followed after its first appearance in the 1992 (the pyramid turned into the "USDA MyPlate" in 2011). While the concepts conveyed by the pyramid, the US government policy, the Big Agriculture industry, the Big Pharmaceutical industry, and the medical community in general remain the foundation of conventional dietary wisdom today, the strategy of eating a grain-based, high-carbohydrate, high-insulin-producing diet has proven to be a disaster of epic proportions.

Today, Americans represent the fattest and least fit population in the history of humanity, and children have a lower life expectancy than their parents for the first time in recorded history. We are experiencing record rates of diet-related conditions such as type 2 diabetes, heart disease, and cancer. As Dr. Doug McGuff observed in his book *Primal Prescription*, if rates of type 2 diabetes continue to climb at today's accelerated rate, the expensive long-term care for this condition is on track to bankrupt the US Treasury by the year 2060! Anti-industrial-oil crusader Dr. Cate Shanahan goes so far as to say that the massive shift from butter to margarine at the government's direction back in the 1970s was a sinister experiment to determine how many people would die from ingesting these toxic but high-profit-margin agents over the ensuing decades.

The Original USDA Food Guide Pyramid

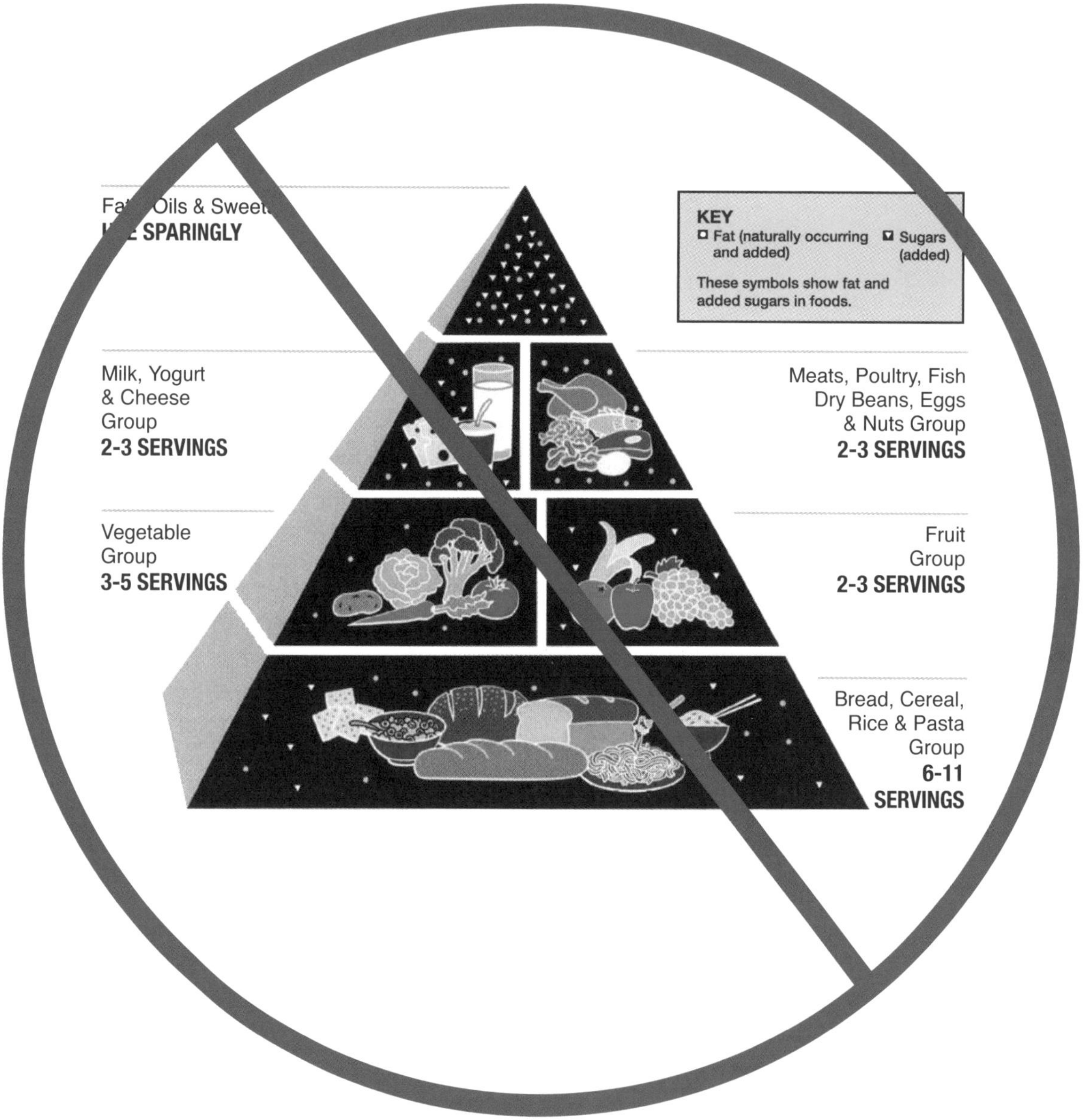

The original USDA Food Guide Pyramid that was first released in 1992.
The most valuable advice on the entire pyramid is definitely: "Use Sparingly!"

The Nose-To-Tail Carnivore Pyramid

It's time to reject flawed and dated conventional dietary wisdom, especially that which has been tainted by special interest lobbying, flawed science, and profiteering interests. It's time to embrace a different pyramid, such as Dr. Paul Saladino's Nose-To-Tail Carnivore Pyramid. Take a look at this simple image and envision the possibilities for a simple, streamlined, extremely nutrient-dense, high-satiety diet:

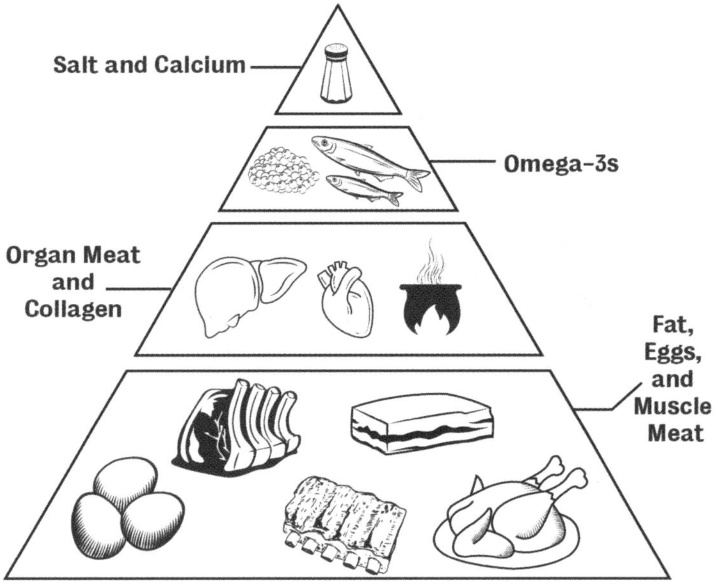

MACROS

- Protein: 0.8 grams to 1 gram per pound of lean body weight
- Fat-to-Protein Ratios
  - Performance: 1.5 to 2 grams of fat per 1 gram of protein
  - Weight gain: 1.5 grams of fat per 1 gram of protein
  - Weight loss: 1 to 0.75 grams of fat per 1 gram of protein

nutritionwithjudy

CARNIVORE MD
PAUL SALADINO, MD

Dr. Paul Saladino is kicking ass, and kicking bag, on the carnivore diet!

HOW HARD CORE FOR MY CARNIVORE?

The predictable question is how strict and exclusive should your carnivore experiment be in order to achieve the desired benefits of improving autoimmune and inflammatory conditions, dropping excess body fat, and locking into an enjoyable, sustainable long-term pattern? Since carnivore is so new and individual response to diet varies tremendously, you must be the ultimate gatekeeper and decision-maker on this one. If you are currently suffering from any kind of chronic condition that might be autoimmune or inflammatory in nature, especially one that has evaded conventional treatment, a strict carnivore experiment for at least 30 days and perhaps longer is certainly warranted. Exclusionary diets allow you to apply a scientific approach and methodical process of elimination to hopefully discover the hidden source of your problems and help you discover the ideal corrective actions to take over the long-term. You have nothing to lose and potentially a health transformation awaiting, so just do it!

If you been frustrated by unsuccessful attempts to shed excess body fat, a strict carnivore phase of at least 30 days and perhaps longer may be the ticket to finally get the job done and move on with your new life and new clothes. When you commit to carnivore, even for a short period of time, you eliminate the dangerous variables of decision fatigue and will power that can derail even the most devoted dieters. When you have to continually resist keto brownies, paleo pancakes and other temptations, or have options to snack on dark chocolate, macadamia nuts, and celery sticks smothered with almond butter, achieving that natural and effortless caloric deficit that prompts fat loss can become more difficult. What's more, the extremely low carbohydrate content and extremely high satiety factor of carnivore meals makes it easier to hang in there on the path to achieving your goals. Again, you have nothing to lose and a ton of satisfaction to gain from finally solving the weight loss puzzle, so just do it!

On the other end of the spectrum, if you report excellent overall health, favorable bloodwork, and optimal body composition, you may be less inclined to a strict approach because there are most likely fewer potential benefits to be gained in comparison with someone who is health challenged. You are certainly welcome to dabble or make a gradual transition over to increased emphasis on carnivore. In the process, you may pick up or discard certain habits in the quest for the optimal eating pattern. Alas, if you are in this peak performer category, you are likely interested in making incremental improvements in all areas of life to obtain a competitive edge. Here again, it may be helpful to obtain a data set of strict carnivore eating for 21-30 days for proper comparison purposes. Review the authors' personal experiences with carnivore (page 32) to get more real-world insight on a strategy that might work best for you.

MORE FRUIT, FEWER VEGETABLES?

The ancestral health message has long been that vegetables should represent the bulk of your dietary emphasis—micronutrient and antioxidant powerhouses to consume in abundance. Meanwhile, restraint with fruit has been recommended due to the higher glycemic response, the potential for overconsumption due to year-round availability, and because fruits have a tendency to be highly *lipogenic* (more easily converted into fat) carbs. Fruit is the most lipogenic carb because fructose, the predominant carbohydrate in fruit, has to be processed in the liver before it can be burned for energy. Since the liver is also where excess carbs get converted into fat, fruit can turn to fat when your glycogen stores are already full. If you are a high calorie burner who frequently depletes glycogen, fruit can become a great choice for the same reason: the liver can easily convert fruit calories into glycogen for storage.

When it comes to the potential reactivity to plant antigens, Dr. Saladino explains that fruit is the least objectionable plant to consume, because it represents the plant's final offering. Go ahead and pick the berry; the plant remains intact and fertile, with thorns to deter invaders into the more protected elements of the plant. In contrast, the most defensible part of the plant (i.e., highest levels of antigens) is the seed—the life force of the plant. Consequently, the most objectionable items to eat in the plant kingdom include whole grains, nuts, seeds, legumes, and whole plants like leafy greens or cruciferous vegetables. Ironically, the popularity of superfoods like broccoli sprouts is due to their high levels of phytonutrients and antioxidants (you may have heard of broccoli sprouts' wonder agent of *sulphoraphane*), but they also have the highest levels of antigens that can cause problems in sensitive people.

If you decide to include some fruit in your carnivore experience in pursuit of dietary variety and enjoyment, choose wisely by emphasizing locally grown, in-season fresh fruit. Realize that with our year-round availability of fruit transported from distant locations and often overly cultivated to be larger and sweeter than its wild counterpart, selectivity is essential. Berries represent the highest-antioxidant, lowest-glycemic fruits. In contrast, tropical fruits like pineapple, mango, and papaya have the lowest-antioxidant, highest-glycemic levels. Enjoy your fresh local berries in the summertime, and strive to consume zero fruit in the wintertime.

CARNIVORE DUDES KITCHEN ARSENAL

Cast-iron skillet: Get a huge one because it's a good arm workout to wield around, and you can make bigger portions and store them for easy reheating. Cast-iron cooking is way healthier than the chemically-treated non-stick pans that will probably give you man boobs and kill your libido. That said, keep in mind we're not doctors, just smarter about nutrition than the vast majority of doctors.

Glass food-storage containers: Get a couple huge containers so you can make big batches and store. Don't use plastic food-storage containers, because the estrogenic compounds in the plastic will shrink your balls and raise your voice pitch. Especially when you microwave plastic.

Stirring spoons, spatulas: Use natural materials like wood and stainless steel. Don't buy plastic shit, and throw your plastic stuff away right now before your balls shrink. Seriously, if you have any nonstick cookware or plastic utensils, you should seriously consider dumping them. If they are peeled, frayed, or otherwise imperfect, you should for sure dump them because they are tainting your meals with toxic chemicals.

Mini food processor: Great for blending liver with ground beef so you can ease into the liver scene if the taste is difficult for you. A free-standing model like the Ninja Food Chopper Express ($25 online) is fast, powerful, easy to use, and easy to clean. You can also get food processor attachments for many blenders.

InstantPot Multi-Use Pressure Cooker: Everyone is getting the InstantPot, so why not you? Indeed, this unit is pretty awesome, and it's touted to replace up to eight common kitchen appliances (pressure cooker, Crock-Pot-style slow cooker, rice maker, egg maker, yogurt maker, steamer, DVR recorder, and more).

Salt: Carnivore enthusiasts require additional sodium and other minerals and electrolytes (potassium and magnesium especially) to recalibrate after the reduction in inflammation and fluid retention throughout the body that happens when you eliminate high-sodium and/or inflammatory processed foods. Get a high-quality natural sea salt or mineral salt (e.g., Himalayan pink salt) instead of the more common iodized salt. Iodized salt is like junk food—it's been heavily processed, stripped of natural trace minerals, and can contain harmful chemicals for anti-clumping or colorizing. In contrast, natural, unrefined salt contains some 90 other supporting minerals and micronutrients and has a natural color of gray or pink. FYI—the only reason salt is refined and stripped of nutritional benefits is to make it look white for consumer appeal. Lame!

Spices: Spices are sourced from plants, so a strict carnivore experience will limit you to shaking only salt on your foods. If you decide to try strict carnivore for 30 days or longer and then allow some spices back into the picture over time, be sure to get organic spices, because conventional spices have been irradiated for consumer safety. This compromises the nutritional quality and generates free radicals in your spice jar. Also, believe it or not, spices can actually go rancid over time, so you should discard anything older than one year.

Cooking oils: Cook with saturated animal fats such as butter, animal fats (lard, bacon grease, duck fat, etc.). These fats are temperature stable for cooking and are a vastly superior choice to the refined high polyunsaturated industrial seed oils, such as canola, corn, soybean, sunflower, safflower, and so forth. These are highly toxic agents that inflict immediate damage at the cellular level when ingested.

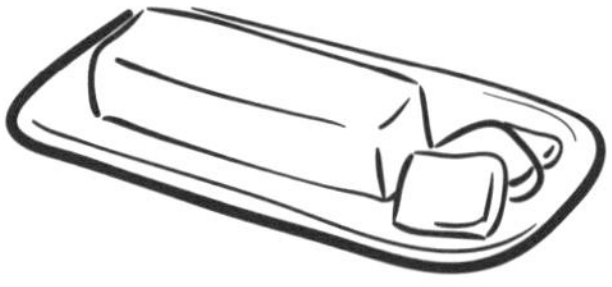

DROPPING EXCESS BODY FAT WITH THE CARNIVORE DIET

Perhaps the most celebrated benefit of the carnivore eating strategy is its tremendous effectiveness for fat reduction. In essence, you have an extremely high-satiety, high-nutrient density, minimal logistics eating strategy that minimizes decision fatigue, eliminates suffering and will power, and turbo charges fat burning like no other diet. You don't have to hassle calorie counting, regimented meal planning or timing, or any other high-stress, unsustainable practice that often leads to backsliding and burnout. Unlike even the wildly popular keto diet, you don't even have to count macros on carnivore. You simply focus your meal options into a nose-to-tail carnivore strategy and watch the fat melt away! Okay, it's not quite that simple, but if you have struggled with the frustrating challenge of dropping excess body fat in the past, carnivore presents an extremely appealing alternative to the obsess, struggle, and suffer approach.

As you may have discovered the hard way, the secret to fat reduction is not as simple as calories in-calories out. Diets usually fail even when you obsessively count calories and work like heck to burn more calories than you eat. If you get depleted and fatigued over time from overly stressful exercise and an under-nourishing diet, you will experience a rebound effect over ensuing months where you naturally move less, work out less, and eat more. The true secret to dropping excess body fat is in *hormone optimization*: giving your body the energy and nutrition it needs to thrive (from high-satiety, nutrient-dense foods ala carnivore), stabilizing your appetite hormones (mainly by cutting processed carbs and industrial oils that compromise fat metabolism), and helping you burn fat and ketones for energy (by fasting frequently and minimizing insulin production). The carnivore diet helps you unlock your magnificent genetic fat- and ketone-burning attributes that have been locked away for years and decades due to carbohydrate-dependency eating patterns.

Dropping excess body fat and excess poundage from inflammation and water retention is extremely easy when your starting point is obesity and/or a heavily processed, grain-based, high-carbohydrate diet. Clean up your act and get moving and you can quickly join the ranks of the before/after photos gracing social media. It's not uncommon for enthusiasts to drop 20 or even 50 pounds in a matter of months. On the other hand, if you are starting with a healthy body composition and eat a nutritious, ancestral-inspired diet, incremental fat reduction becomes increasingly difficult and requires a precise approach. Follow these seven tips to leverage the carnivore eating strategy to the fullest for the specific goal of fat reduction:

Tip #1: Emphasize Fasting

Being highly fat- and keto-adapted means that you are easily able to skip meals and maintain high energy levels and cognitive performance. Mark Sisson describes it as follows: "You can get your next meal off your plate, or off your butt and thighs—your choice." While eating a delicious steak and eggs breakfast is certainly a winning carnivore strategy, body fat must become your primary option for fuel until you reach your goal weight. Obviously, whenever you experience true hunger, you can enjoy satisfying meals. Be highly aware of when you have eaten enough to feel satisfied and stop there instead of having pig-out sessions.

If you are struggling with skipping meals and waiting patiently for the next one, consider having some coffee in the interim—especially for morning fasting periods. Coffee may help curb your appetite in addition to increasing energy and alertness. There is nothing like staying productive to quickly pass the time until your next delicious meal! You should consider two meals a day to be the absolute maximum necessary for any health human, especially if you are trying to drop excess fat. Try to eat 1.5 meals per day on several days of the week to ensure you quickly progress to your body composition goal. Once in a while, try and eat just one meal per day, going from a 4 p.m. early dinner to another early dinner the following day. However, be sure that your meal-skipping/meal-reduction goals happen naturally and comfortably. Never force extended fasts that compromise your physical or cognitive performance or put you in a foul mood. Instead, honor the *WHEN* strategy: When Hunger Ensues Naturally, it's time to eat! What you will likely discover when following a carnivore eating pattern is the ability to skip meals and still feel alert and energetic.

Be highly aware of when you have eaten enough to feel satisfied

Tip #2: Temporarily Increase Protein and Minimize Added Fat

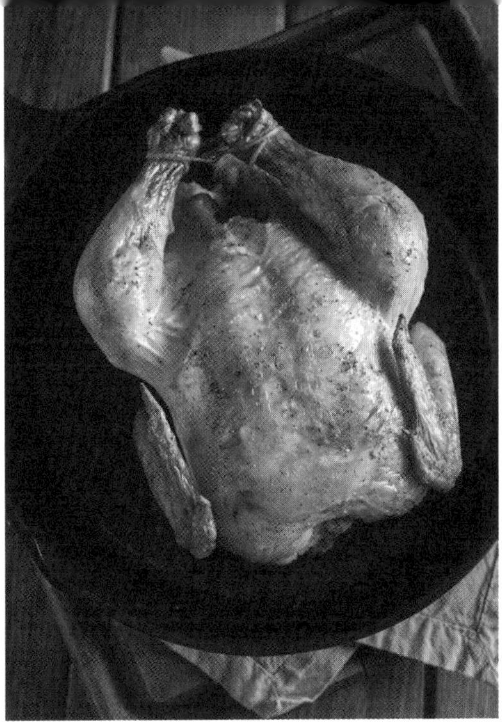

While keto/carnivore/ancestral eating patterns celebrate natural, nutritious fat as a dietary centerpiece, make a little tweak in the name of body fat reduction by emphasizing high-protein foods like grass-fed beef and cutting back on the purposeful inclusion of extra fat in your diet. Rather than adding lots of tallow, butter, or cheese to your meals—simply stick with the whole-food fats already found in your meats and eggs. You can also enjoy leaner cuts of chicken and turkey, plenty of eggs (the yolk is fatty, but the nutrition is too important to skimp), and high-protein dairy such as low-fat cottage cheese and Greek yogurt. Once you have hit a good maintenance weight, higher-fat carnivore foods like oily, cold-water fish, extra egg yolks, and fattier cuts of meat can be emphasized for optimal hormonal health and energy. Remember, reducing added fat and increasing protein is a temporary tweak to achieve fat reduction.

Will has had success with himself and his clients with this higher-protein approach. For fat loss, he recommends that you aim for a 2:1 ratio of protein grams to fat grams (i.e., eating 200 grams of protein to 100 grams of fat). You can implement a 2:1 ratio for a few days before incorporating a higher fat 1:1 ratio day (i.e., eating 150 grams of protein to 150 grams of fat) and repeating the cycle. When you bump up your animal protein intake, you will naturally default to a lower daily caloric intake and accelerated fat burning. Then after 2-3 days of this, a slightly higher-fat day will help reduce any hormonal or immune stresses that can arise from aggressive fat reduction.

Coupled with a sensible exercise program featuring comfortably paced cardio along with regular brief, explosive high-intensity sprints and strength sessions, you can expect to get that six-pack back that's gone missing for a while. While this high-protein, lower-fat spin on carnivore is a little controversial, Will emphasizes that this is a short-term strategy designed for fat reduction. Over the long run, certain individuals may not respond well to a diet that is both strict low-carb and low-fat (others may be just fine). Personal preference and sustainability should be the guiding principles in the long run.

Tip #3: Cut the Carbs!

While the carnivore diet defaults you into extremely low carbohydrate intake, the matter deserves additional attention when you are trying to reduce excess body fat. Even a minor carbohydrate snack, such as a designer energy bar or sweetened drink from Starbucks, will halt fat burning, stimulate an insulin response, and kick you over into glucose-burning mode. It's difficult to escape from this pattern once carbs are introduced into the picture. When you stay focused and committed to a carnivore pattern, you will experience the incredible effects of appetite regulation, elevated dietary satiety, and finally a freedom from carb cravings that have probably been there for your entire life.

Realize that you don't have to be extreme or unreasonable about carb avoidance. Eggs, oysters, and Greek yogurt are still just fine, even though they contain a few grams of carbs per serving. What we're talking about is shutting down those celebratory binges that you allow after a hard workout or during weekend festivities. When you get those final few pounds of fat off your body, it will be easy to keep the fat off—even if you loosen up your dietary guidelines over time. This is due to the body's assorted homeostatic set point mechanisms—the same hormonal processes that make it difficult to drop excess body fat in the first place even when you start exercising more and tightening up your diet.

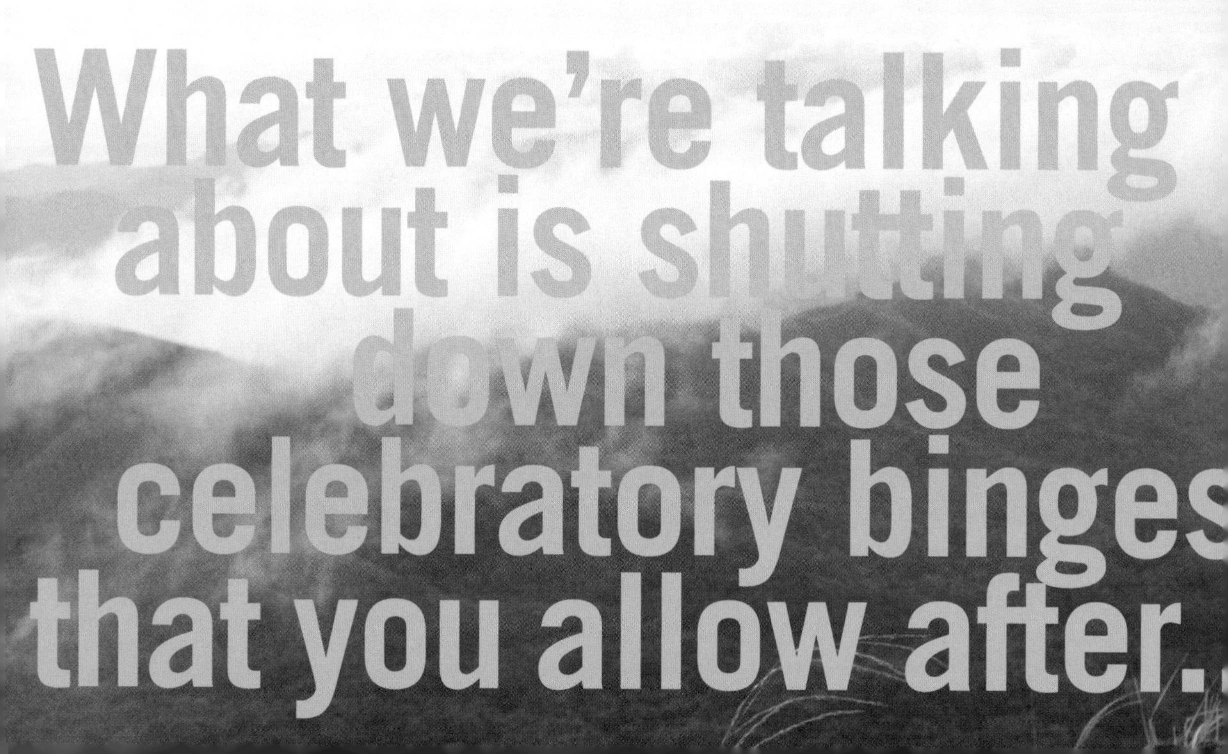

Tip #4: Conduct High-Intensity Workouts

Perform brief, explosive sprints and/or full-body functional strength exercises 2-3 times per week. The idea here is to optimize hormone function and send the genetic signals to shed excess body fat with a properly designed workout. The key is to go hard and go home with an explosive workout of 30 minutes or less. This will ensure that you don't overstimulate stress hormones or deplete muscle glycogen, nor trigger sugar cravings and overeating in the hours after the session.

Unfortunately, most fat-loss enthusiasts royally screw this up by performing prolonged, high-calorie-burning, exhaustive workouts. Can you say "boot camp," "CrossFit," "HIIT class," or "Tuesday night track workout?" The intentions here are honorable: bust your ass in the gym or at the track to drop body fat. The problem is it simply doesn't work. A scientifically validated concept called the *compensation theory* suggests that your body reacts to exhaustive workouts by burning fewer calories at rest, doing less activity, spiking appetite, and increasing fat storage in the hours after your killer session. These are all genetically programmed survival mechanisms to protect you from the perceived life or death threat of energy depletion.

Instead of the losing pattern of draining your tank and over-compensating with huge meals and incessant snacking, give your body the optimal genetic stimulation of brief, high-intensity sessions that are invigorating instead of exhausting. Perform explosive lifts that work the largest muscle groups, such as squats, bench press, deadlift, overhead press, barbell rows, and pullups. Use heavy resistance with low reps, take extensive rest between sets, and finish the workout in less than 30 minutes. For sprinting, efforts should last between 10 and 20 seconds, with extensive rest intervals (a minute or longer) that replenish cellular energy and enable every effort to be truly explosive. Complete between 4-10 reps and that's all you need to generate the hormonal signaling for rapid fat reduction. These types of workouts will ensure you get the burst of adaptive hormones like testosterone and human growth hormone in the bloodstream but avoid the overproduction of stress hormones that you will cause problems in the ensuing hours and days.

Tip #5: Incorporate Comfortably Paced Cardio

Cardiovascular exercise will help boost the fat-loss process, provided you do it at a comfortable heart rate of "180 minus age" or below in beats per minute. For example, a 35-year-old would conduct cardio workouts at a heart rate of 145 beats per minute (180 – 35 = 145) or below. As with the brief, high-intensity workouts, it's not the calorie burning that matters here, but rather the stimulation of your fat burning mechanisms that provides the true value. Hard to believe, but a hike to the radio towers, a casual pedal down the beach bike path, or a mellow elliptical session as you watch TV in the gym can be of greater benefit to fat loss than the cardio hammer sessions that emphasize glucose burning instead of fat burning. Again, this is due to the optimal hormonal signaling of aerobic (fat burning) exercise and avoiding the depleting effects of overly stressful cardiovascular sessions.

The key to ensure that your cardio sessions are effective is to honor Dr. Phil Maffetone's "180 minus age" formula for maximum aerobic heart rate and keep things easy and comfortable. If you don't have a heart rate monitor, get an inexpensive unit like the Polar F1 online for around 30 bucks (or the newer FT1 for 60 bucks). It's very easy to exceed your aerobic maximum during a routine workout, because the intensity level is so comfortable. If you are exercising in the aerobic zone, you should be able to carry on a normal conversation without getting winded or be able to breathe entirely through your mouth. Resist the temptation to go a little faster to burn more calories and feel like you are getting a "real" workout. When you exceed aerobic maximum, you start to burn a greater percentage of glucose (and less fat) and also prompt stress hormone production. After a slightly too difficult cardio session, you will drift into glucose burning and tend to eat more calories, especially carbs. Slow down to burn fat, and of course hit the weights, or sprints, hard at your other workouts. Choose walking, hiking, bicycling, swimming, light jogging if you are fit, or cardio machines at the gym, and enjoy the relaxing and hormone-optimizing effects of a properly paced cardiovascular session.

Tip #6: Optimize Sodium, Mineral, and Electrolyte Intake

Deficiencies in sodium, minerals, and electrolytes often become a hidden struggle for low-carb enthusiasts. It's common to attribute fatigue, brain fog, poor workout performance, sugar cravings, and headaches to cutting carbs from your diet, failing to recognize how adding a little more high-quality sodium can generate big improvements. Your sodium, mineral, and electrolyte needs are also increased when you are trying to shed excess body fat, as dropping fat is yet another stressor to the body.

Organ meats get high marks in the area of minerals and electrolytes, but when you are strict carnivore and avoid potassium superstars like sundried tomatoes and avocado, and don't eat as much organ meat and bone-in cuts of meat as would be ideal, consider a supplement regimen to ensure your success.

Review the "Supplement Recommendations for a Carnivore Diet" on page 43 for details, and strongly consider the electrolyte bomb as detailed on page 45 with collagen, sodium, glycine, potassium, magnesium, creatine, and L-carnitine. Make absolutely sure that you add 5-10 grams of high-quality sodium each day to your foods and beverages. Also pay close attention to magnesium, as experts believe that the vast majority of modern humans (even healthy eaters) are magnesium deficient. Taking magnesium at night can help with sleep. You can take capsules or choose a topical spray, since magnesium is absorbed efficiently through the skin.

SALT FLATS, BOLIVIA

Tip #7: Manage Stress Levels

The worst thing you can do when trying to lose fat is to try too hard to the extent that you introduce too many stress factors into the picture. Acknowledging that fasting, calorie restriction, and carbohydrate restriction are all stressors to the body, it's imperative that you minimize your overall life stress levels during your fat-reduction efforts. In particular, you must be absolutely sure that you don't over-exercise, as this will push you back in the direction of sugar cravings and carbohydrate dependency. You must strive to increase all forms of general everyday movement, because prolonged periods of stillness at your desk, commuting, and enjoying digital entertainment will shut off your fat burning genes and also promote carb dependency.

Also realize that if you are sleep deficient, it will destabilize your appetite and satiety hormones to the extent that you will be prompted to overeat and be more likely to store those excess calories as fat. Take care of yourself every single day, prioritizing healthy eating, general movement, high-intensity workouts, excellent sleep habits, and sufficient downtime from hectic, hyperconnected modern life. You got this!

THE FINAL FRONTIER—GETTING DOWN TO SINGLE-DIGIT BODY FAT

Struggling to get down to single-digit body fat is typically an ordeal of extreme calorie restriction, chronic hunger, irritability, fatigue, and brain fog. Even if you do reach your goal and snap a photo for social media virility…I mean virality, you will eventually experience backsliding, burnout, and recalibration to a higher body fat percentage. Cool Dudes ain't about that, so please consider a sensible and more appealing alternative. If you have established an excellent baseline fitness level and eat a clean, nutritious, fat-adapted diet, the goal of a head-turning physique is within your reach. However, you have to adopt the correct approach, because this is an extremely challenging endeavor. As you have probably already discovered, the body simply does not like to let go of those last few pounds of fat when you are already lean and fit.

First things first: It's important to realize the imagery you see from fitness leaders and celebrities is edited and airbrushed to perfection, rather than cameo snapshots of reality. It's a common practice to get what's called the "money shot" for a magazine cover, runway show, physique contest, or film role, and then quickly rehydrate, replenish, and return to a significantly less impressive appearance that is the true everyday baseline. Professional bodybuilders and Tour de France cyclists alike routinely pack on 10-20 pounds of extra weight during the off-season. This increased fluid retention and fat storage actually serves as an important recovery mechanism from their extreme and unsustainable training and cutting regimens of the peak season.

Google "Lauren Fleshman Keeping It Real" for a revealing and perspective-altering article from this Olympic runner about the distorted imagery we see in magazines and social media. You'll be shocked at the disparity between photos taken of Fleshman during the same week: first, on an activewear fashion show runway with six-pack glistening; next, some less flattering cameo images taken during a track practice, coupled with Fleshman's quip, "Everyone has thigh cheese."

Speaking of keeping it real, it's important to recognize that getting your body fat down to elite physique levels might get you lots of props on social media, but it can easily run counter to one of your strongest hardwired human genetic drives: reproductive fitness. This is especially true for females, where ample body fat levels (definitely beyond magazine cover specs!) are necessary for fertility. When pursuing any physique goal, it's advisable to adopt a big picture perspective where you strive for energy, strength and power, endurance, and overall health and happiness in addition to a lean physique. If you feel like you have to compromise some of these attributes in order to make further body fat reductions, consider pursuing more sensible and realistic goals. Indeed, body composition results may vary according to your individual genetics. For example, those with equatorial ancestry generally have a genetic predisposition to carry less body fat than those with ancestry from the higher latitudes. Granted, anyone can achieve low body-fat, but the process may be more difficult based on your genetics and whether you are a natural ectomorph (slender), mesomorph (muscular), or endomorph (heavy set).

For reference on body-fat percentages, males in the single-digits—nine percent or below—represent elite status. This equates with a six-pack in full glory and distinct muscle groups (quadriceps, calves, triceps, lats) and vascularity (veins on skin surface) visible throughout the legs and upper body. Females at 15% or below represent elite status. They are tight and toned even through the hips, butt, thighs, and abdomen—areas where body fat typically accumulates even in fit females. Males at 15% and females at 22% body fat are considered fit and athletic. They are not carrying any excess around, but they have less visible definition than those in the elite category. Males over 25% and females over 32% are typically considered to be unfit and overfat. At these levels, the recommendation is to make immediate diet and exercise modifications to at least get below these thresholds.

Now that we've helped you adopt a healthy perspective, let's also acknowledge that you have the right to shoot for the stars and go after the lean, toned, sexy body that you dream of. It's going to require a temporary sacrifice of the pleasures and indulgences of eating delicious meals that are a centerpiece of modern culture. In many ways, you will feel like you are pursuing a lonely goal, because you will routinely be taking a step back and watching while others celebrate indulgent modern life at social gatherings or at home on the couch watching a movie. Great opportunities for mindfulness training! You'll make the wonderful discovery that it's possible to achieve goals, feel better about yourself, and still enjoy life without stuffing your face at every opportunity.

William works hard every day to maintain his single-digit physique and assist others in making breakthroughs with his Primal Body program (primalbody.co). Here is what he says about making that final incremental progress from good to great:

> "Remember to keep fasting as the centerpiece and only eat when you're really hungry. Focus on consuming lots of protein daily (lean beef, chicken and turkey, eggs, Greek yogurt, low-fat cottage cheese—I don't ever limit protein) and keeping fat just high enough to feel satiated. When you are really going for it, you'll want to trim or drain the fat off the fattier meats you consume. Choosing foods with a high protein-to-energy ratio will accomplish satiety at far fewer calories than other foods.
>
> Also, stay away from the carbs, dude! Again, this is a temporary and highly focused strategy to reach a lofty goal; no leaking or rationalizing allowed. Conduct brief, high-intensity sessions and plenty of comfortable cardio. Optimize your intake of sodium and electrolytes, sleep like a champ, and make sure you are pursuing physique goals at a time in life when stress levels are low. It's just too hard to try for elite body composition goals when life is hectic.
>
> If you are really working hard and can't seem to get a break, I mean a breakthrough, try increasing the degree of difficulty of one of your high-intensity strength training sessions each week. The body needs to be shocked to move off of your set point, and epic workouts are the most effective way to do this. Lastly, an occasional fat refeed meal once or twice a week can help reset your fat burning hormones and keep you moving in the right direction."

THE AUTHORS' CARNIVORE STRATEGIES

Brad

In early 2019, I was intrigued after listening to podcasts with Dr. Paul Saladino and Dr. Shawn Baker and decided to try out this carnivore thing. Since I wasn't suffering from any acute health conditions, I didn't see the need to be super strict. However, once the concept took hold in my mind, I noticed that I quickly and naturally drifted into greater alignment with a nose-to-tail carnivore pattern. I felt incredibly well-nourished and satiated by fasting until 12 noon and then preparing a large meal emphasizing the highest-quality animal foods, including much more emphasis than ever before on organ meats.

Beyond feeling satisfied on fewer total meals and much less snacking (fewer options, less desire to eat between robust carnivore meals), I noticed a significant improvement in my digestive function, which is to say that I didn't notice *anything!* There was no gas, bloating, transient minor pain, or loose pipes in association with challenging workouts. These symptoms have been part of my life for so long that I have come to view them as "normal."

Perhaps of most interest, my joint commitment to go carnivore and fast until 12 noon enabled me to quickly drop eight pounds of excess body fat in exactly three months. I attribute this quick and easy success to the natural focus and discipline engendered by my morning fast and narrowed menu options. (Okay, I let dark chocolate hang in there to the extent that I joked to friends that I was following the C&C diet!) We forget how easy it is to get derailed from our goals and best intentions by freedom, abundant choice, and the indulgent and decadent cultural influences we are surrounded by daily. When we are thrown into the mix of daily life without unwavering rules and guidelines in place, it's easy to experience decision fatigue, depletion of will power, and a consequent unraveling of our best-laid plans.

After my fat reduction goal was achieved, I decided to relax my commitment to both carnivore and to fasting until 12 noon. This was mainly in the interest of enjoying life and directing my precious assets of focus, discipline, and will power into other areas (e.g., staying off email when trying to write a book!). I have experienced numerous lasting effects and behavior changes accordingly, summarized as follows:

- **Carnivore for Life:** Nose-to-tail carnivore foods of the highest quality will continue be the central focus of my diet. After all, these are the foods that drove human evolution for 2.5 million years and are the most complete and nutrient-dense foods on earth.

- **Efficiency:** The high-satiety and low-insulin-stimulating effects of carnivore have resulted in more fasting, a narrower average daily eating window, and easier shopping and meal preparation.
- **Plants:** My favorite plant foods are drifting back into the picture, such as: fresh seasonal fruits, homemade kombucha, high-cacao percentage dark chocolate, nuts and nut butters, sundried tomatoes, and avocado/guacamole. I don't go looking for massive piles of plant matter to eat in the name of health as I did previously. If I'm served some delicious broccoli slathered in butter, I'll eat it. But I'm not at the farmer's market piling my basket with every conceivable plant species in the name of health. This is especially true for consuming raw greens, which seem to cause digestive disturbances for most everyone when consumed in abundance, such as a giant green smoothie.
- **Fruit:** After 12 years of restricting fruit and consuming vegetables in abundance per primal/paleo recommendation, I have basically flip-flopped the picture. I consume more fruit and fewer vegetables (see **More Fruit, Fewer Vegetables?** on page 18). However, I am extremely selective about my fruit and limit my intake to fresh, seasonal fruit of the highest quality. Per our genetic expectations, I consume zero fruit in the winter months.
- **Organs:** I have made a firm commitment to up my organ meat game. Now I head straight to the butcher and request grass-fed liver, heart, kidney, oxtail, and more. I drink flavorful bone broths of the highest quality from Bonafide Provisions. And I supplement intently with my Male Optimization Formula w/Organs—MOFO! (bradkearns.com/mofo).

Brian

After about three years of strict ketogenic eating, I decided to try a carnivore experiment—not much of a stretch from my existing keto pattern. The experience has been a revelation, just when I thought there was not much more I could do to optimize my diet. Here are some of the key takeaways:

- **Simple and Pragmatic:** While I'm not strict carnivore, I have drifted into what I call a "produce-free lifestyle." This has vastly simplified my grocery shopping, as well as cut down on my grocery bill and food waste. Even when I was keto and eating lots of vegetables, I always felt that my produce could possibly be a ripoff from a "dollars per caloric and nutritional contribution" standpoint.
- **Decision Fatigue:** I find that the fewer choices I have to make about my diet, the more likely I am to be satisfied with those choices. A person's disposition toward their diet is just as important as the diet itself. Are you stressed and anxious trying to find "allowable" foods? Are you burdened by the chore of tracking macros? The less mental energy required to follow a diet, the more likely it will be sustainable, enjoyable, and successful.
- **Fat Loss Hack:** I've found that a high-protein diet (approximately 55 percent protein) with minimal fat is the quickest path to fat loss for me. This greatly reduces my appetite and also makes the thermic (calorie burning) effect of protein significant enough to move the needle. Granted, I don't do this all the time, and I sort of view this "increase protein–reduce fat" as a "hack." If I'm not trying to lose fat, I'll typically consume about a gram of protein per pound of bodyweight per day. This brings me down to around 30 percent of total calories from protein. In these routine maintenance times, the rest of my calories will come from fat, or sometimes whatever my wife cooked up that night. Yes, including carbs!
- **Plant Strategy:** I still include foods from the plant kingdom that add flavor and enjoyment, but generally these items are shelf-stable and don't go rotten in the fridge. These include herbs, spices, natural local honey, low-calorie condiments with clean ingredients from Primal Kitchen, canned tomato paste, nuts and nut butter (as recipe ingredients, but never as stand-alone snacks), and gluten-free beer in the evenings. I also do just fine with high-fat dairy, so I include Greek yogurt, raw milk, and whey protein powder.
- **Offspring:** My carnivore experience has changed the way I feed my kids. No more fighting with them to "eat their vegetables!" Animal foods are inherent-

ly tasty due to their fat content, but kids basically have to be either tricked into eating vegetables by adding lots of fat or by using assorted coercion and bribery strategies. Enough of that—seems like questionable parenting strategies anyway. My mission is to front-load my kids (when they're hungriest!) with high-quality animal foods like beef, eggs, and sardines. Once I feel that we've checked that box, the kids can obtain the rest of their calories from easy to eat, energy-dense foods that can fuel activity and growth. I'm pretty agnostic where these calories come from as long as they're not highly inflammatory or containing nasty stuff like high fructose corn syrup and industrial seed oils. With my kids, white rice, fruit, and macadamia nuts are typical offerings.

- **Refeeds:** I don't plan cheat days or refeeds or anything like that, but I live by the motto of "life gives you refeeds." Diversions from my mostly carnivorous diet are usually social occasions like kids' birthdays, weddings, or backyard BBQ's with friends. My goal is to keep my everyday diet so dialed that I have the wiggle room to eat like a regular dude at social celebrations.
- **Conscience:** I'd like to leave you with one last point. There is no diet that doesn't have a certain degree of loss and suffering attached to it. Whether you're vegan or carnivore, we all have blood on our hands and have to acknowledge that our being on this planet comes with a cost. Rather than try to reduce that cost to zero, I encourage folks to look at the other side of the equation—what you're adding back to the world. All life feeds on life. Try to live a life worthy of taking it.

William

I can't believe it's been over two years since I started carnivore in mid-2017! My carnivore journey started on a whim, intended as a short-term experiment to see if I could get a quick improvement in body composition. It's turned into not only my default dietary strategy, but a way of life. My typical daily routine is to awaken super early and hit the gym by 5 a.m. for some hard work. Around 10 a.m. or 11 a.m., I'll often have a light lunch of salmon slices, hard-boiled eggs, or leftovers from the previous evening's dinner. On other days, I'll fast until 5 or 6 p.m. if I'm busy and didn't do an extreme workout that day. Generally, I wait until I experience true sensations of hunger before consuming calories. I feel more focused and productive at work when I'm in a fasted state, including not having to bother with meal preparation. Around 5 or 6 p.m., I'll enjoy my main carnivore-inspired meal of the day.

I enjoy sharing carnivore with others to solve the incredible challenge of dropping excess body fat, because carnivore simply works—and without the fuss and stress of counting macros or limiting portions. Here are some of my favorite takeaways from my ongoing carnivore journey:

- **Fasting:** Fasting has become an instinctive tool I use—rather than a discipline that I follow. I will simply fast until I'm hungry. No specific windows around that, but it's very easy to complete the occasional 16- or 23-hour fast when I'm feasting on nutrient-dense foods and utilizing ketosis.
- **Body Fat:** I maintain single-digit body composition naturally, thanks to the incredibly high-satiety meals, minimized appetite, and stable energy and cognitive function all day long.
- **Macros:** Within the carnivore paradigm, I've done extensive experimentation to discover the best way to both remain lean and get stronger in the gym. Moderating fat intake and bumping up the protein a bit has been very successful for me. The satiating nature of protein means I never have to worry about portion control nor calorie counting.
- **Nutrient Density:** From my baseline of red meat and eggs, I make a concerted effort to include nutritional powerhouses like bone broth, beef liver and other organs, additional egg yolks, and additional protein (both collagen and whey).

- **Hard-Core:** Overall, I'm pretty strict carnivore, but I do allow a few plants into the picture in the name of enjoying my meals, including coffee, spices, and low-sugar condiments like Primal Kitchen catsup and steak sauce. Fruits and vegetables are all but absent from my plate, save for some occasional fresh seasonal berries.
- **Cheat/Treat:** Once or twice a month, I enjoy an occasional day of indulgence where I break from routine and celebrate life! Yep, you'll even find some pizza and ice cream cameos on my Instagram page (@williamshewfelt).

CHANGE YOUR LIFE EATING CARNIVORE DUDES RECIPES!

Ditching carbohydrate dependency, honing metabolic flexibility, and exploring the potentially awesome benefits of a nose-to-tail carnivore dietary strategy is only part of the picture of living a long, healthy, happy life. The Cool Dudes encourage you to adopt a comprehensive approach where you not only eat well, but exist on the planet as a kind, well-adjusted, happy, stress-balanced, creative, and energetic person. Here is a quick look at big picture health objectives to aspire to as a Cool Dude:

Move Frequently: Increasing all manner of everyday movement is now seen by experts as even more important that structured workouts. Avoid prolonged periods of stillness that compromise fat metabolism and promote sugar cravings.

Cardio: Engage in at least a few hours a week of structured cardiovascular workouts at a comfortable "180 minus age" in beats per minute. This is where you enjoy maximum fat oxidation with a minimum amount of glucose burning. This is a surprisingly easy pace, meaning you typically have to slow your jogging or cardio machine pace to get better at burning fat.

Strength Training: Brief, intense strength training sessions boost anti-aging hormones, improve brain function, and make you generally more energetic and confident. Do sweeping, full-body functional movements like squats and deadlifts. Go hard and go home, making each set explosive and with excellent form. Take plenty of rest between sets to avoid cumulative fatigue that leads to burnout, sugar cravings, and performance plateaus.

Sprinting: The ultimate primal workout helps turbo-charge fat burning and makes you more resilient to all other forms of exercise and general everyday stress. All you need is to conduct a handful of brief, explosive sprints once a week or so. Do just 4-10 reps lasting 10-20 seconds, with extensive rest intervals so that you deliver a consistent quality of effort on every sprint. Deliver a quality sprint workout just once a week and you can expect huge fitness and body composition breakthroughs.

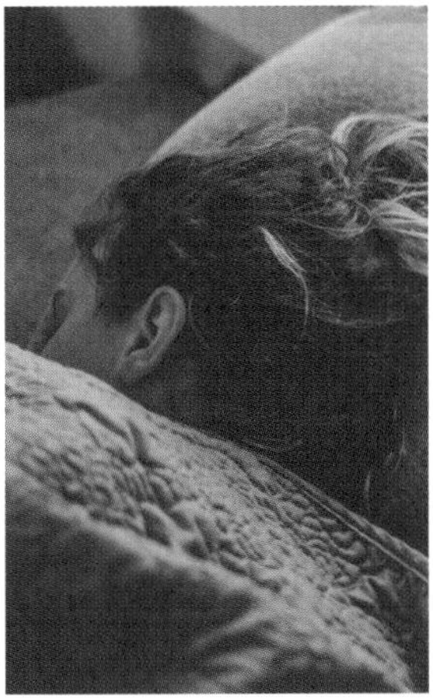

Sleep: Getting adequate sleep must become your number-one health priority. Sleep deficiency will destroy your devoted attempts at dietary transformation and push you back toward carb dependency and fight-or-flight excess, and also crash your testosterone levels.

Focus on two objectives: minimizing artificial light and digital stimulation after dark, and creating a sleep sanctuary. Get your screen use out of the way early in the evening, and then wind down with relaxing activities like reading, evening strolls, or Borat sexy time hey hey. Your bedroom should be minimalist and free from clutter, cool (60-68F; 15-20C), and completely dark at night.

Cold Exposure: If you want to escalate your game to level 9 badass, consider a morning cold therapy regimen. Start with two minutes of cold at the end of your showers, then escalate to a morning chest freezer cold plunge. Brad spends several minutes in 34-38F (1-4C) water every morning doing a meditative deep breathing sequence that builds mental resiliency and focus and gives a dramatic boost in the focusing and motivation hormone norepinephrine. Search YouTube for "Brad Kearns, Unfrozen Caveman Runner," to be further regaled about his rewarming runs and sprint workouts.

Quit Being a Dickhead to Your Girlfriend/Wife: John Gray, Ph.D., the number-one bestselling selling relationship author of all-time with his *Men Are from Mars, Women Are from Venus* book series, dispensed life-changing advice during his *Get Over Yourself* podcast interview with Brad: "Males, you must not speak if you have an negative emotional charge. If you are too sensitive, emotionally needy, and demanding, it's a turn off. Instead, take some 'cave time' and engage in testosterone-boosting activities (workouts, watching sports, handyman projects). Your primary biological role is to protect your woman, most importantly from your own anger! When you say, 'I feel hurt,' this is death to a relationship. Don't talk—how many times do I have to tell you this!" (Seriously, the dude said all that, and he knows his shit!)

The Carnivore Dudes encourage you to quit making excuses and start living the healthy, fit active lifestyle that brings your energy, happiness, and longevity. Educating yourself about nutrition and choosing the healthiest possible foods is a huge element of healthy living, but these efforts can become seriously compromised if you don't pay attention to the big picture items.

Carnivore advocate Shawn Baker, MD (Instagram @ShawnBaker1967), 52, is a world record setting rower. He eats four pounds of meat per day to fuel his ambitious training regimen.

Dr. Art DeVany

FASTING ON CARNIVORE

Dr. Art DeVany, one of the forefathers of the ancestral health movement, author of *The New Evolution Diet*, and a highly credible source on account of still being ripped at 82 years old, says that "We are perhaps most human when we don't eat... because we turn on genes that are geared toward stress resistance, repair, and maintenance." Fasting is such a healthy process that it's been incorporated into many religions as a means of cleansing, purification, and attaining spiritual enlightenment. Fasting has been scientifically validated to deliver profound anti-inflammatory, anti-aging, and immune benefits, as well as promote the natural internal cellular detoxification called *autophagy*, and the desirable programmed death of dysfunctional and pre-cancerous cells known as *apoptosis.* These processes get compromised by a high-sugar, high-stress life, accelerating the aging process and increasing your disease risk factors.

When your body is in a fasted state, you will lower insulin, burn through liver glycogen, and accelerate fat burning. Levels of adrenalin-like hormones and growth hormone both increase, leading to the sharpened mental state many experience while fasting. All these processes are accelerated when you conduct a fasted workout and continue to fast afterward. Alas, these strategies should be considered advanced, because you have to be fat-adapted to experience the intended benefits of fasting. If you attempt to fast or engage in extreme calorie restriction when you are still carbohydrate dependent, you will trigger the fight-or-flight response when you attempt to fast. Because of your chronically elevated insulin levels and poor fat-burning capabilities, you will engage the process of *gluconeogenesis*—the conversion of lean muscle tissue into glucose—to get the calories you need. Over time, this will lead to exhaustion, burnout, and a compensatory response of stuffing your face to replenish your depleted brain and body.

Even if you are an experienced fat burner, it's important to adopt a strategic approach to fasting and never over-do it. Realize that fasting is a stressor to the body. If you combine too many stressors (lack of sleep, too much caffeine, overly stressful exercise patterns, insufficient daily calories, inferior nutrient density, stress with work and personal relationships), you will default into fight-or-flight mode and upregulate cortisol production instead of fat burning. A good rule of thumb to follow is to fast until you feel hungry, then eat instead of suffer!

When consuming a carnivore-style diet low in carbohydrates and rich in protein, natural fats, and vital nutrients, you will be in touch with your true hunger rather than blood sugar highs and lows. Over time, you will be able to trust your body to tell you when to eat and how much. You will experience lots of time in the fasted state naturally, and you'll be able to derive all of the intended benefits.

Another warning to heed relating to fasting is: *Don't snack!* Snacking on any kind of food, even something that's high-protein or high-fat and low-carb, still causes an insulin release and shuts down fat burning accordingly. If you experience some mental difficulty with hanging in there for long fasting periods, try William's recommendation of drinking green tea, coffee, or saltwater to help you pass the time. Some research suggests that green tea and coffee can boost fat-burning potential, and some added high-quality natural mineral salt will ensure that you don't experience energy dips caused by electrolyte and mineral deficiencies.

Another warning to heed relating to fasting is: Don't snack!

SUPPLEMENT RECOMMENDATIONS FOR A CARNIVORE DIET

An intelligently formulated nose-to-tail carnivore eating strategy will largely negate the need for supplements because you are consuming the most nutrient-dense and highly bioavailable foods on the planet. As Dr. Paul Saladino, author of *The Carnivore Code*, reminds us, our shared biology with the animal kingdom means animal foods require less effort to digest and assimilate than plant foods. For example, liver is rich in the incredibly important vitamin A in its fully formed state, known as retinol. In contrast, the beta-carotene you obtain from colorful plant foods like carrots and sweet potatoes must be converted to vitamin A through a more elaborate biochemical and metabolic processes. Saladino cites a study that it takes 21 units of beta-carotene to equal the biological value of one unit of retinol!

Alas, as with any dietary strategy, you are not going to get an A-plus every day for your food choices. Some carnivore enthusiasts have been criticized for relying on steaks every day with insufficient variation and hence potential shortcomings in their micronutrient profiles. Consequently, here are some suggestions for the most relevant and potentially beneficial supplements for carnivore eaters:

Calcium

If you are eating primarily muscle meat and not many bone-in cuts of meat or bone broth beverages, you may benefit from supplemental calcium powder. Here are some recommended products:

- Whole-bone calcium in powdered form
- Bone marrow in freeze-dried capsule form (BradKearns.com/mofo)
- Bone broth: homemade or a high-quality store-bought variety. Be sure your product is gelatinous when refrigerated and has "bones" in the ingredient list.
- Bony fish such as canned salmon or sardines
- Whey protein in powdered form. Look for micro-filtered whey protein isolate, and stay away from products with artificial sweeteners.
- Fermented dairy: grass-fed cottage cheese, Greek yogurt, high-quality hard cheese (e.g., raw milk cheese or aged cheese)

Liver

Grass-fed beef liver is in the running for the most nutrient-dense food on the planet and will cover many of your nutritional bases if you give it regular attention in your diet. Unfortunately, liver is often not a fan favorite, and it can be difficult to source grass-fed liver. Here are some ideas to up your liver game:

- Desiccated grass-fed liver capsules or tablets: AncestralSupplements.com offers 100% grass-fed liver from the pristine pastures of New Zealand for maximum purity and nutrient value.
- Organ meat burgers: If you dislike the taste of liver, puree raw liver with ground beef or lamb and make burgers. You'll enjoy the taste and turbocharge a routine burger into a superfood!

Omega-3s

Oily, cold-water fish are the richest dietary source of omega-3s, offering vastly superior values to any other food category. Strive to feature sardines, salmon, salmon roe, oysters, and other sustainably caught fish in your carnivore experience. If you are weighted more toward ribeyes than marine life, consider taking a pharmaceutical-grade fish oil supplement. Choose a high-quality product free from additives and impurities, and stay away from the huge inexpensive omega-3 containers at the discount stores. Store your product in the fridge, consume the bottle quickly, and discard any bottle with a rancid smell. Follow the label serving size recommendations, as taking extra omega-3 can be counterproductive.

- Pharmaceutical-grade fish oil with EPA and DHA forms of omega-3 listed on label, and designations such as "wild caught" and "sustainable/environmentally friendly." Do not consume an inferior omega-3 supplement, as they can easily go rancid and deliver a dose of free radicals!

Sodium, Minerals, and Electrolytes

When you depart from a grain-based, high-carbohydrate, high-processed foods diet, you will experience a significantly increased need for sodium and other important minerals and electrolytes. The reason is that cleaning up your diet results in a reduction of inflammation and water retention in cells throughout the body, and thus a disruption of your existing electrolyte balance. Second, ditching processed foods that are extremely high in sodium compared to any natural food will reduce your overall sodium intake. Third, dropping excess body fat puts additional strain on your hydration-sodium-electrolyte-mineral balance. All this is good news, but you have to implement a sound replenishment strategy.

Your first objective out of the gate is to add 5-10 grams (1-2 teaspoons) of additional sodium per day using a high-quality natural mineral salt, Himalayan pink salt, or ancient sea salt. Sodium is the gatekeeper to the retention of other minerals and electrolytes, so low sodium will cause further depletion problems. Make a practice of adding a couple pinches of natural salt to every cup of liquid that you drink, and gradually consume your salted hydration beverages over a long period of time. These measures will ensure that the tissues throughout your body will be optimally hydrated. In contrast, if you slam a jug of plain water right after a sweaty workout, you'll likely disrupt your sodium balance and excrete the extra water instead of absorbing it.

Make a habit of shaking additional salt onto all of your meals to get your five grams covered with ease. If you are exercising regularly, strive to increase your intake to 7-10 grams per day. Your kidneys do an excellent job at maintaining proper hydration, sodium, and electrolyte balance in your bloodstream at all times, so you have minimal risk of overdoing it. However, if you under-consume sodium and the others, you can mess up thyroid and adrenal function and experience fatigue during workouts and at rest. There are a few other extremely important minerals and electrolytes to supplement with when you are doing carnivore, especially if your intake of organ meats, bone-in cuts of meat, and bone broth is slacking a little.

Dr. Paul Saladino recommends this custom-for-carnivore mineral/electrolyte bomb. You can easily source these products at a good health food store or online (amazon.com or bulksupplements.com). Make things easy on yourself by ordering the following items in powdered form, combining them together in the recommended proportions in a new container, then mixing them in a heaping scoop in water—a great post-workout recharge!

- 1 scoop (~20 grams) collagen protein
- 3-5 grams of natural mineral salt, sea salt, or pink salt
- 3-5 grams of glycine powder
- 1 gram of potassium powder
- 400 mg magnesium citrate powder

Dudes performing strenuous workouts also like to add:

- 5 grams creatine powder
- 5 grams L-glutamine powder

Collagen

Our ancestors consumed animals in nose-to-tail fashion, affording them a bunch of beneficial compounds that are scarce in the modern diet that overly emphasizes muscle meat and completely ignores some of the most nutritious parts of the animal in the joints and connective tissue. Connective tissue is rich in collagen protein, which nurtures the health of your own connective tissue throughout the body. Amazingly, dietary or supplemental collagen has a *heliotropic* effect in your body—it travels into the areas where it is most needed, such as a brittle joint or tendon. Collagen also is believed to support the integrity of your gut lining with a highly touted "heal and seal" effect. Collagen is rich in amino acids like proline and glycine, which can promote good sleep by acting as inhibitory neurotransmitters.

Make the best effort you can to include organ meats and bone-in cuts of meat in your carnivore meals, or you can hardly call yourself a true carnivore. It's that important! Bone-in meats and bone broth also deliver vastly more calcium, magnesium, phosphorous, sodium, and other important micronutrients in comparison to muscle meats. In the mean time, cover your bases and any potential shortcomings by supplementing with bone broth and a high-quality collagen supplement:

- Collagen hydrolysate
- Collagen peptides
- High-quality, gelatinous bone broth

AND NOW... FOR THE RECIPES>

For your convenience, we have categorized the recipes as Eggs & Dairy, Fish, Meat, Offal, and Poultry. Numerous recipes feature ingredients from more than one category. In these cases, we tried to categorize a recipe according to their predominant ingredient. Hopefully you will cruise through each section and get into a rhythm of making your favorites frequently and also experimenting with new stuff whenever inspiration strikes! Good luck. And feel free to stray from the script if you come up with a creative twist; that's how most of these recipes came to be.

EGGS & DAIRY

MAKES 1 SERVING

COOKING TIME:
10 MINUTES

BODYBUILDER'S OMELET

This omelet has a great protein-to-energy ratio for those looking to shed body fat.

1. Heat frying pan on medium-high heat.
2. Crack eggs and mix with egg whites and salt.
3. Melt tallow in pan.
4. Add eggs to pan and make omelet.
5. When omelet is almost ready, add cottage cheese to one side and fold inside.

2 large eggs

8 large egg whites

1 cup (225 g) low-fat cottage cheese

1 tablespoon (15 g) beef tallow

Sea salt

MACRONUTRIENTS PER SERVING: CALORIES: 586 FAT: 31 G CARBS: 12 G PROTEIN: 67 G

MAKES 1 SERVING

COOKING TIME:
15 MINUTES

BRAUNSCHWEIGER & ANCHOVY EGG "PIZZA"

Because anything the shape of a disc is a pizza.

2 large eggs

2 ounces (57 g) mozzarella or parmesan cheese (high in leucine!)

2 ounces (57 g) Braunschweiger or liverwurst

6 (15 g) anchovy pieces (pack a lot of flavor)

Italian or Greek seasoning

1 tablespoon (15 g) beef tallow or butter

1. Beat eggs and season with Italian or Greek seasoning.
2. Heat cast-iron skillet to medium heat and melt butter/tallow.
3. Preheat broiler or toaster oven.
4. Add eggs to pan and cook until bottom is set, about 2 minutes.
5. Flip without breaking your egg disk.
6. When slightly brown and crispy on both sides, remove from heat and top with half the cheese, then the Braunschweiger and anchovies, then top with other half of cheese.
7. Move pan/pizza to oven and broil for 2-3 minutes until cheese is melted.
8. Top with additional Greek or Italian seasoning.

Optional:
Add other toppings to your liking, such as pickled pepperoncini peppers.

MACRONUTRIENTS PER SERVING: CALORIES: 613 FAT: 49 G CARBS: 2 G PROTEIN: 39 G

MAKES 2 SERVINGS

COOKING TIME:
20 MINUTES

CARNIVORE SAUSAGE EGG McANDREW-MUFFINS

We just turned McMuffins® inside out and on the ground with this recipe. Get rid of that crusty bun and use nutrient-dense eggs to piece together juicy pork sausage instead.

2 tablespoons (30 g) beef tallow

½ pound (227 g) pork breakfast sausage

4 large eggs

Sea salt

½ cup (120 ml) water

Primal Kitchen Spicy Ketchup

1. Use 3 ½-inch biscuit cutters to make sausage patties.
2. Heat a pan over medium heat and melt 1 tablespoon (15 g) tallow.
3. Fry the sausage patties 2-3 minutes per side.
4. Transfer patties to plate.
5. To make egg "buns," whisk eggs with sea salt.
6. Add another of tablespoon (15 g) of tallow to heated pan.
7. Place the biscuit cutters in the pan, and pour one egg's worth of beaten egg into each biscuit cutter.
8. Add water to pan, but outside the egg molds.
9. Turn heat to low and cover the pan.
10. Cook the eggs covered for about 3 minutes.
11. Transfer eggs to a paper-towel.
12. Assemble egg buns and sausage sandwiches.
13. Serve with Primal Kitchen Ketchup.

MACRONUTRIENTS PER SERVING: CALORIES: 568 FAT: 48 G CARBS: 0 G PROTEIN: 31 G

MAKES 2 SERVINGS

COOKING TIME:
30 MINUTES

CHEESY HARD-BOILED EGGS & BACON

This is a delicious entrée that you can tempt your non-carnivore friends with. When they're asking you concernedly if the cholesterol will clog their arteries—show them your six pack, and carry on.

6 large eggs

2 ounces (57 g) shredded cheese

4 slices bacon

Himalayan pink salt

Black pepper

1. Place 6 eggs in a large pot and cover with 1 inch of cold water. Cover with lid.
2. Bring water to rolling boil, then remove from heat source. Let eggs sit for 8-10 minutes with lid on.
3. Remove eggs from water and immediately place in icy water for 2-3 minutes.
4. Peel the eggs and cut in half vertically.
5. Pan-fry 4 slices of bacon. Sprinkle with shredded cheese.
6. Once firm, slice bacon and stick in yolks. Season with salt and pepper as desired!

MACRONUTRIENTS PER SERVING: CALORIES: 369 FAT: 27 G CARBS: 2 G PROTEIN: 27 G

MAKES 1 SERVING

PREP TIME:
5 MINUTES

COTTAGE CHEESE PROTEIN BOMB

Sometimes carnivore on-the-go can be a little tough, so here's a cheap & easy snack that will keep you full and nourished! If you do well with dairy that is…

1 4.4-ounce (125 g) tin of sardines, packed in water

2 cups (324 g) cottage cheese

2 tablespoons (14 g) bacon bits

1. Mix it all together in the cottage cheese tub.
2. Enjoy!

MACRONUTRIENTS PER SERVING: CALORIES: 685 FAT: 33 G CARBS: 20 G PROTEIN: 83 G

MAKES 1 SERVING

PREP TIME:
5 MINUTES

COTTAGE CHEESE TUNA SALAD

Another meal with super high protein-to-energy ratio to help you get shredded.

2 4-ounce (113 g) cans of tuna

2/3 cup (108 g) low-fat cottage cheese

1 tablespoon (15 g) yellow mustard

1 tablespoon (15 ml) lemon juice

***Optional*: ½ teaspoon (2.5 g) garlic powder**

1. Drain water from tuna.
2. Combine all ingredients in a bowl.

MACRONUTRIENTS PER SERVING: CALORIES: 370 FAT: 7 G CARBS: 10 G PROTEIN: 69 G

MAKES 1 SERVING

COOKING TIME:
5 MINUTES

CREAMY CARNIVORE COFFEE

Adding butter, coconut oil, and MCT oil to your coffee is so 2017. Leave that keto kraziness behind and try this Creamy Carnivore Coffee! It'll add some micronutrients from egg yolks, some electrolytes from the pink salt, some skin and joint support from the collagen, a little extra fat for energy from the heavy cream...and that good ol' kick only coffee can provide. Coffee is usually considered a "gray area" in the carnivore diet—many carnivore dieters include it and some don't. Assess your personal tolerance!

1 raw large egg yolk

1 tablespoon (15 ml) heavy cream

1 tablespoon (9 g) unflavored hydrolysate gelatin

Himalayan pink salt

10 ounces (300 ml) dark roast coffee (whichever brewing method you prefer)

1. Add 1 tablespoon (15 ml) heavy cream and 1 raw egg yolk to 10 ounces (300 ml) of hot coffee. Blend with hand blender for 20-30 seconds or until frothy.
2. Add 1 tablespoon (9 g) collagen/gelatin and just a pinch of pink salt to coffee and continue blending for 10-15 seconds more. Enjoy!

MACRONUTRIENTS PER SERVING: CALORIES: 133 FAT: 10 G CARBS: 2 G PROTEIN: 9 G

MAKES 6 SERVINGS

COOKING TIME: 60 MINUTES

CURLEY BOYS' BREAKFAST SQUARES OR MUFFINS

Make a huge batch and then you can heat up servings for a quick morning meal on the go. But don't eat and text and drive. Don't even text and drive. Muffins are cool, but just use a baking pan if you are lazy, then cut out an appropriate serving each day. PS – The Curley boys are real brothers who used to inhale these muffins on wild outdoor global adventures—before they got real jobs, houses, and wives. Now they inhale them before a hard day's work schlepping Salomon shoes.

1 pound (454 g) grass-fed ground beef, lamb, or buffalo

2 cups (200 g) chopped vegetables: onion, mushroom, pepper, kale, spinach, broccoli bits, tomatoes

12 pastured large eggs

***Optional*: sun-dried tomatoes, feta or mozzarella cheese, bacon (previously cooked)**

***Spices:* Real Salt or other quality natural salt, mixed spices from Costco or Trader Joes, or, order Cool Dudes mixed spices online (just kidding, we don't sell spices)**

1. Preheat oven to 350F (175C).
2. Sauté mixed veggies in 1 tablespoon (15 g) of butter or oil (avocado, coconut, or olive).
3. Chop up the ground meat and fry in different pan, or same pan if you are lazy.
4. Break the egg shell and drop contents into bowl. Repeat 12 times. Mix it together.
5. Mix all ingredients together and pour into baking pan. If you want muffins, borrow a muffin tin from a female neighbor, friend, or family member. Spray each hole with nonstick. Fill each hole halfway with eggs, then top off with meat and veggie mixture
6. Bake at 350F (175C) for 20-25 minutes, or until you see a little browning of top layer.

MACRONUTRIENTS PER SERVING: CALORIES: 297 FAT: 19 G CARBS: 4 G PROTEIN: 28 G

MAKES 1 SERVING

COOKING TIME:
0 MINUTES

DUDES' FASTING BREAKFAST

Fasting is a great way to hone metabolic flexibility and turbo-charge fat burning. Ancestral health forefather Dr. Art DeVany says, "We are perhaps most human when we're not eating." That's when immune, metabolic, and cognitive function are optimized.

1. Wake up and don't eat any food. While people use lame terms like "juice fast" or "brown rice fast," fasting means not consuming any calories. Instead, drink a tall glass of water, herbal tea, or black coffee when you wake up, and then see how long you can sustain peak energy, mood, and cognitive function without eating. Don't struggle or fight through authentic signals of hunger, because this may kick you into a fight-or-flight response and gluconeogenesis. In this state, because you haven't eaten and aren't yet an expert at burning stored body fat, your body breaks down lean muscle tissue to make glucose to supply your energy needs.

2. If you feel your stomach growlin', this is a sign of true hunger and the up-regulation of the prominent appetite-stimulating hormone *ghrelin*. As Dr. Cate Shanahan likes to say, "Ghrelin gets your stomach growlin'." Experiencing hunger is a cue to sit down for a nutritious carnivore-aligned meal such as an omelet. As you progress further with carnivore-friendly diet and lifestyle patterns, you will be able to naturally and comfortably last longer in the morning without food and feel great. If you can make it from say, an 8 p.m. dinner the previous evening until 12 noon the following day, you earn a gold star for fat- and keto-adaptation. The Dudes' Fasting Breakfast is literally one of the healthiest recipes in this entire book.

MACRONUTRIENTS PER SERVING: CALORIES: 0 FAT: 0 G CARBS: 0 G PROTEIN: 0 G

MAKES 2 SERVINGS

COOKING TIME:
10 MINUTES

EGGS-IN-A-HOLE BURGERS

Before you donate your entire shot glass collection, save just one to use for this delicious burger recipe. Ok, maybe save two, so you can cook twice as many of these at a time.

¾ pound (342 g) ground beef

2 large eggs

Sea salt

1 tablespoon (15 g) beef tallow

1. Season ground beef with salt and form into two large patties.
2. Use a shot glass and create a hole in the centers of the burgers.
3. Heat a frying pan or cast-iron skillet to medium-high heat.
4. Cook burgers about 3 minutes per side until brown and crisp on the outside.
5. Carefully drop eggs into holes, reduce heat to medium-low, and cover until egg white is set and yolk is still a little runny.

MACRONUTRIENTS PER SERVING: CALORIES: 462 FAT: 33 G CARBS: 1 G PROTEIN: 39 G

MAKES 10 SERVINGS

COOKING TIME:
1 HOUR 5 MINUTES

FABULOUS FREE-FOR-ALL FRITTATA

This will serve a grand gathering for brunch as easily and deliciously as anything you can possibly imagine. You know this whole book is all about making cooking quick, easy, and fun, but it's hard to top this frittata for ease and deliciousness. You chop up a bunch of stuff, mix up some eggs, pour it into the dish, and 30 minutes later you have a colorful centerpiece meal. No offense, but this recipe blows the doors off all the trendy brunch places in a hipster city near you. You'll have this whole thing completed in around 45 minutes, same as the typical Sunday wait time at the hipster spot. The next time someone says, "Epic party last night dude; let's walk down to {fill in the blank} for brunch!", just say, "Forget that, I'll just make the Fabulous Free-for-All Frittata!"

18 slices bacon

18 large eggs

3 ounces (85 g) sliced high-quality cheese, such as raw milk

1 cup (240 ml) organic heavy whipping cream

1 medium (160 g) onion, chopped

3 cups (575 g) broccoli, finely chopped

2 cups (300 g) red bell peppers, finely chopped

2 cups (60 g) spinach

Salt, pepper, and mixed spices

1. Preheat oven to 350F (175C).
2. Cook the bacon on a cookie sheet for 30 minutes or until done to perfection.
3. While the bacon is cooking, mix the chopped vegetables, eggs, cream and spices together in a bowl.
4. Crumble the bacon and combine it with the egg mixture.
5. Pour in a 9 x 13" baking pan greased with butter and bake at 350F (175C) for 35 minutes or until a knife comes out clean and/or until the top starts browning.
6. Turn off the oven and add thin strips of cheese to the top of the frittata. Allow the cheese to melt, and serve.

MACRONUTRIENTS PER SERVING: CALORIES: 331 FAT: 47 G CARBS: 6 G PROTEIN: 17 G

MAKES 2 SERVINGS

COOKING TIME:
15 MINUTES

GIRONDA STEAK AND EGGS

The breakfast (and dinner) of champions. Vince Gironda's "Maximum Definition" diet consisted of steak and eggs twice a day with a high-carb meal thrown in every 4 or 5 days.

1 pound (454 g) sirloin steak

Sea salt

2 large eggs

1 tablespoon (15 g) beef tallow or butter

1. Preheat grill or grill pan (grilling is ideal since it doesn't require any additional cooking fat for the steak).
2. Season steak with sea salt.
3. Grill steak for about 10 minutes total for medium-rare.
4. While steak is cooking, heat a second pan on medium heat and melt a bit of tallow or butter.
5. Remove steak from grill and allow to rest for 5 minutes.
6. While steak is resting, fry 2 eggs to your liking.

Optional:
Use hard-boiled eggs.

MACRONUTRIENTS PER SERVING: CALORIES: 577 FAT: 40 G CARBS: 0 G PROTEIN: 52 G

MAKES 12 SERVINGS

COOKING TIME:
2 HOURS

HONEY MERINGUE KISSES

Because no cookbook is complete without a little dessert.

4 large egg whites

1 cup (240 g) honey

Sea salt

1. Refrigerate a mixing bowl until cold.
2. Preheat oven to 225F (107C).
3. In a different mixing bowl, combine egg whites, honey, and a generous pinch of sea salt.
4. Set bowl over a medium-sized saucepan filled with a couple inches of water. Bring water to a low boil. While water is boiling, begin to whisk egg whites and honey. Whisk for 3 minutes until they've turned into a nice, white froth.
5. Pour frothy egg mixture into cold bowl and continue whisking until the mixture is shiny and has stiff peaks. Note that hand whisking might take 20-30 minutes. Use a stand mixer with a whisk attachment for ease and speed.
6. Line baking sheet with parchment paper.
7. Using a tablespoon, scoop mixture onto baking sheet. Bake for about 90 minutes.
8. Turn off oven, but leave baking sheet inside, allowing kisses to dehydrate. For best results leave overnight and eat the next day.

MACRONUTRIENTS PER SERVING: CALORIES: 69 FAT: 0 G CARBS: 18 G PROTEIN: 1 G

MAKES 1 SERVING

COOKING TIME:
10 MINUTES

MEATY OMELET

Here's another easy staple! This is a delicious breakfast basic that should be nailed on carnivore!

1 tablespoon (15 g) butter

2 sliced pork sausages

4 large eggs

½ cup (63 g) shredded cheddar cheese

1. Set pan to medium heat. Melt 1 tablespoon (15 g) of butter in the pan. Add sliced pork sausages and brown slightly. Remove them.
2. Whisk the eggs in a bowl and pour into the pan, tilting the pan to evenly coat with the eggs.
3. After a couple of minutes, you should see bubbles. Gently lift the edges of the omelet with a spatula to let the uncooked part of the eggs flow toward the edges and cook. Continue cooking for 2-3 minutes or until the center of the omelet starts to look dry
4. Place the cheese in the middle of the omelet and spread the sausage on top (in the center of the omelet). Using a spatula gently fold one edge of the omelet over.
5. Let the omelet cook for another two minutes or until the cheese melts to your desired consistency. Slide the omelet out of the skillet and onto a plate. Enjoy!

MACRONUTRIENTS PER SERVING: CALORIES: 747 FAT: 56 G CARBS: 2 G PROTEIN: 47 G

MAKES 2 SERVINGS

COOKING TIME: 20 MINUTES

NORI
BREAKFAST BURRITO

Nori makes for a great tortilla substitute, especially when used with eggs where the moisture from them helps soften and seal the nori wrap together. We like to hide nutrient-dense Braunschweiger in ours.

5 large eggs

4 ounces (113 g) Braunschweiger

8 sheets of nori

Tapatio/Cholula hot sauce

***Optional:* butter or cooking oil**

1. Cook Braunschweiger in a frying pan until browned. The sausage might have enough fat content to cook itself and the eggs in, depending on what kind you use, but if not, add some butter or cooking oil.
2. Add the eggs and scramble.
3. On your countertop, lay out 4 nori sheets in a big square but overlapping in the middle. There should be enough eggs and sausage to make two "noritos" of 4 sheets each.
4. Pour eggs in a line down the middle and attempt to wrap like a burrito.
5. Serve with hot sauce.

MACRONUTRIENTS PER SERVING: CALORIES: 403 FAT: 30 G CARBS: 8 G PROTEIN: 27 G

MAKES 1 SERVINGS

PREP TIME:
5 MINUTES

OLD SCHOOL BODYBUILDER PROTEIN SHAKE

In the 1950s-1970s, bodybuilders had lean, muscular, athletic physiques. They followed a high-protein, moderate-fat, low-carb eating style—very similar to a carnivore diet. A true old school protein shake would have consisted of some milk powder, heavy cream, raw eggs, and probably whole milk. We're going to modify a bit!

2 tablespoons (30 ml) heavy cream

1 scoop (15 g) stevia-sweetened whey protein

2 tablespoons (18 g) unflavored hydrolyzed collagen

3 raw large egg yolks

Pinch Himalayan pink salt

1. Start with 6 ounces (170 ml) of water. Add 1 scoop (15 g) whey protein and 2 tablespoons (18 g) hydrolyzed collagen. Shake in a protein-shaker bottle.
2. Add 3 raw egg yolks and 2 tablespoons (30 ml) heavy cream. Add a pinch of pink sea salt for electrolytes. Shake again and enjoy!

MACRONUTRIENTS PER SERVING: CALORIES: 339 FAT: 24 G CARBS: 2 G PROTEIN: 26 G

MAKES 1 SERVING

PREP TIME:
5 MINUTES

PRE- OR POST-WORKOUT GREEK GOD YOGURT

1 ½ cups (300 g) FAGE plain, non-fat Greek yogurt

5 ounces (150 ml) cold water

2 tablespoons (18 g) gelatin powder

1 teaspoon (5 g) raw honey to taste

Pinch sea salt

This recipe allows you to get some carbs in around training if you so desire. It's also a good method to "volumize" your Greek yogurt to stretch that yogurt tub and your wallet a bit further.

1. In a bowl, mix Greek yogurt with water and gelatin.
2. The gelatin should thicken the mixture. Stir until water disappears and mixture thickens up to roughly what it was before diluting with water.
3. Add a pinch of sea salt and 1 teaspoon (5 g) raw honey (or to taste or based on how much carbohydrate you want) and enjoy!

MACRONUTRIENTS PER SERVING: CALORIES: 226 FAT: 0 G CARBS: 16 G PROTEIN: 44 G

MAKES 1 SERVING

COOKING TIME: 2 HOURS

RAW MILK GEL-O

¼ cup (60 ml) cool water

¼ cup (60 ml) very hot water

1 tablespoon (9 g) gelatin powder

1 ½ cups (360 ml) raw milk

***Optional*: honey to taste**

Many wise men have said not to drink your calories, so here's a great way to consume the nutritional powerhouse that is raw milk without drinking it. If you're not averse to whey protein powder, you could use a scoop or two of whey and sub the raw milk for cool water.

1. Pour cool water in a medium-sized bowl and add gelatin.
2. Stir and let it thicken.
3. Add ¼ cup (60 ml) of very hot, nearly boiling water and mix.
4. Add raw milk (and honey to taste) and stir.
5. Put in the refrigerator, covered for at least 2-3 hours.

MACRONUTRIENTS PER SERVING: CALORIES: 265 FAT: 14 G CARBS: 18 G PROTEIN: 20 G

MAKES 6 SERVINGS

COOKING TIME:
45 MINUTES

SAUSAGE AND EGG CUPS WITH LIVERWURST SPREAD

Make a big batch of these and keep them in the fridge for a few days at a time. Silicone muffin liners are easy to clean, so you'll be more likely to whip these up on the regular.

1 pound (454 g) ground pork or beef sausage

6 large eggs

4 ounces (113 g) liverwurst

2 ounces (57 g) cream cheese

Sea salt

1. Preheat oven to 350F (177C).
2. Take a muffin tin and line the insides with ground meat. Cover the sides and leave room in middle for egg.
3. Beat 6 eggs in a bowl with sea salt.
4. Pour egg mixture into the middle of each cup.
5. Bake for about 30 minutes.
6. Mix liverwurst, cream cheese, and any desired seasonings in a bowl.
7. Let muffins cool. Top with liverwurst/cream cheese spread.

MACRONUTRIENTS PER SERVING: CALORIES: 331 FAT: 26 G CARBS: 0 G PROTEIN: 22 G

MAKES 1 SERVING

COOKING TIME:
10 MINUTES

SMOKED MACKEREL AND SALMON ROE OMELET

The best way to get in more seafood is sometimes by stuffing it into eggs! These omelets are delicious; take our word for it.

2 tablespoons (30 g) salmon roe

1 6.7-ounce (190 g) tin of mackerel

4 large eggs

½ tablespoon (7 g) butter

Pink Himalayan salt

1. Melt ½ tablespoon (7 g) butter in medium-low heat pan. Whisk 4 eggs together in bowl, adding any desired spices and pink salt. One pan is hot, add eggs to pan. Let cook for 3-5 minutes, until center and outsides begin to harden.
2. Add mackerel and salmon roe in the center of omelet. Fold omelet over carefully using spatula and let cook for 1-2 minutes. Flip again and let cook until firm.
3. Enjoy!

MACRONUTRIENTS PER SERVING: CALORIES: 887 FAT: 67 G CARBS: 0 G PROTEIN: 71 G

MAKES 12

TOTAL TIME:
5-20 MINUTES
(DEPENDING IF EGGS
ARE HARD-BOILED
ALREADY)

SMOKED OYSTER DEVILED EGGS

There are a lot of ways to make deviled eggs these days, but how often do you see smoked oysters on the menus of those hip restaurants? Be the first and whip these up for your friends. See how cool carnivore is?

6 large eggs

1 3.5-ounce (85 g) tin of smoked oysters, packed in olive oil

***Optional*:**
1-2 tablespoons yellow mustard

1. Hard-boil eggs.
2. Peel and cut in half.
3. Scoop out yolks and place in a bowl.
4. Drain oil from tinned smoked oysters and mix with yolks using a fork.
5. Mix until consistency is smooth, adding optional mustard.
7. Use a spoon to add yolk/oyster mixture back into egg whites.

MACRONUTRIENTS PER SERVING: CALORIES: 61 FAT: 5 G CARBS: 1 G PROTEIN: 4 G

MAKES 1 SERVINGS

COOKING TIME:
20 MINUTES

STEAK AND *EGG DROP SOUP*

Soup is a great food to eat while dieting since it increases the volume of a meal with liquid and makes it seem like you've eaten more.

6 ounces (170 g) steak (any variety), cut into bite-sized pieces

2 cups (480 ml) boxed beef bone broth

2 large eggs

1 tablespoon (15 ml) fish sauce

1 tablespoon (15 g) beef tallow

Sea salt

1. Melt tallow in a saucepan on high heat.
2. Cut beef into bite-sized pieces and season with sea salt.
3. Cook beef, browning all sides.
4. When beef is cooked, add bone broth and reduce heat to a simmer.
5. Add fish sauce.
6. Beat eggs.
7. Stir the pot of beef and broth in one direction to create a whirlpool and then slowly stream in the beaten eggs to create the egg "ribbons."

MACRONUTRIENTS PER SERVING: CALORIES: 684 FAT: 46 G CARBS: 0 G PROTEIN: 63 G

MAKES 1 SERVING

COOKING TIME:
15 MINUTES

STEAK AND *EGG TACOS*

We recommend using leftovers (if you have any) from Brian's 10-Minute Sirloin Steak (page 158) for this recipe.

4 large eggs

6 ounces (170 g) leftover cooked sirloin steak

1 tablespoon (15 g) beef tallow/butter

Sea salt

¼ cup (15 g) chopped cilantro

1 tablespoon (15 g) minced onion

Tapatio hot sauce

1. Beat 4 eggs with some sea salt.
2. Heat a larger non-stick pan on medium-high heat. (The size of the pan will decide the size of your tortillas. Something like a wok can create something the size of a burrito.)
3. Add tallow or butter to grease the pan and prevent sticking.
4. Add eggs and rotate pan in a circle so eggs come up the side of the pan, creating a very thin layer.
5. Just before eggs start to burn, use a spatula to flip the tortilla and cook the other side.
6. Remove from pan and place on plate.
7. Cut up steak into small, bite-sized pieces and spread out across the middle of egg tortillas.
8. Top with diced onion, fresh cilantro, and Tapatio hot sauce.

MACRONUTRIENTS PER SERVING: CALORIES: 802 FAT: 55 G CARBS: 1 G PROTEIN: 70 G

MAKES 1 SERVING

COOKING TIME:
10 MINUTES

STEAK OMELET

Got some leftover steak but not enough for a whole meal? Whip up this easy steak omelet!

4 large eggs

2 ounces (57 g) New York strip steak

1.5 ounces (43 g) brie cheese

1 tablespoon (15 g) butter

1. Set pan to medium-low heat. Melt 1 tablespoon (15 g) of butter in the pan. Whisk the eggs in a bowl and pour into the pan, tilting the pan to evenly coat with the eggs.
2. Gently lift the edges of the omelet with a spatula to let the uncooked part of the eggs flow toward the edges and cook. Continue cooking for 2-3 minutes or until the center of the omelet starts to look dry.
3. Place the brie cheese in the middle of the omelet and spread the steak on top (in the center of the omelet). Using a spatula gently fold one edge of the omelet over.
4. Let the omelet cook for another two minutes or until the cheese melts to your desired consistency. Slide the omelet out of the skillet and onto a plate. Enjoy!

MACRONUTRIENTS PER SERVING: CALORIES: 663 FAT: 53 G CARBS: 0 G PROTEIN: 44 G

MAKES 4 SERVINGS

COOKING TIME:
15 MINUTES

T-BONE STEAK AND EGGS

You like some good dairy? You a fan of protein? Of course, you are...that's why you're here. This meal is guaranteed to put hair on your chest and give you an Adam's apple. Or at least make you very, very full.

1 pound (454 g) T-bone steak

4 large eggs

½ cup (81 g) cup low-fat cottage cheese

½ cup (125 g) plain, low-fat Greek yogurt

Sea salt

Black pepper

½ tablespoon (7 g) butter

1. Set grill to medium-hot.
2. Pat steaks dry and sprinkle all over with sea salt and pepper.
3. Grill steak for 4 to 5 minutes before flipping. Grill until medium-rare. Plate the steak and tent with foil.
4. Heat cast-iron skillet or frying pan to medium-low. Melt ½ tablespoon (7 g) butter.
5. Crack 4 pastured eggs in the same pan and let the egg whites harden. Season with sea salt and black pepper.
6. Flip the eggs after 3-5 minutes. Let cook for another 2 minutes. Plate the eggs.
7. Add ½ cup (81 g) cottage cheese and ½ cup (125 g) Greek yogurt to plate. Enjoy!

MACRONUTRIENTS PER SERVING: CALORIES: 340 FAT: 21 G CARBS: 2 G PROTEIN: 35 G

MAKES 1 SERVING

PREP TIME:
10 MINUTES

VINCE GIRONDA SOFT-SERVE ICE CREAM

Vince Gironda had something called the "Hormone Pre-Cursor Shake" that was basically a lot of raw eggs and heavy cream. This is a more conservative take that blends nicely into something resembling soft serve ice cream.

1 large egg

1 ounce (30 ml) heavy cream

2 scoops (40 g) stevia-sweetened whey protein

2 tablespoons (18 g) unflavored hydrolysate collagen

¼ teaspoon (1.25 g) sea salt

2 cups (480 g) ice cubes

***Optional*: honey to taste**

1. Crack egg and add to high-speed blender.
2. Add heavy cream, sea salt, 1 scoop (20 g) of whey and collagen.
3. Add 1 cup (240 g) of the ice.
4. Start blending on lowest speed for a minute or two.
5. As ice becomes smoothly blended, add another cup (240 g) of ice.
6. Once that's smoothly blended, add second scoop (20 g) of whey.
7. Blend until consistency is smooth and thick.

Optional:
Add honey to taste.

MACRONUTRIENTS PER SERVING: CALORIES: 396 FAT: 20 G CARBS: 9 G PROTEIN: 48 G

MAKES 1 SERVING

COOKING TIME:
15 MINUTES

WEST AFRICAN SARDINE OMELET

Great way to hide sardines if you don't totally love sardines.

4 large eggs

1 4.4-ounce (125 g) tin of sardines, packed in water

1 habanero pepper

2 tablespoons (30 g) beef tallow

1 teaspoon (5 g) sea salt

***Optional*: ¼ cup (40 g) sliced onion**

***Optional*: sub salt for Maggi Boullion or straight MSG seasoning**

1. Crack 4 eggs into a blender with a tin of sardines and a habanero pepper.
2. Blend on low for 30 seconds.
3. Heat tallow in a pan on medium-high heat.
4. When pan is crackling hot, add onion and cook until translucent.
5. Add egg/sardine mixture and cook until one side is starting to get golden crispy.
6. Flip omelet and cook other side.
7. Fold over and serve.

MACRONUTRIENTS PER SERVING: CALORIES: 738 FAT: 53 G CARBS: 4 G PROTEIN: 58 G

MAKES 1 SERVING

PREP TIME:
5 MINUTES

YO-TATOES

1. In a small bowl or cup, mix Greek yogurt with two egg yolks.
2. Mix in enough sea salt (and optional seasonings) to make it taste "good."
3. Add in one packet of gelatin, which should "solidify" the mixture and make it the texture of mashed potatoes.
4. Serve with steak, or double or triple the recipe to eat as a stand-alone meal.

Most people want the creaminess that traditional mashed potatoes provide, not the actual insulin-spike that they also are known for. This fast yogurt recipe gets you the creamy without the notorious food coma.

⅓ cup (80 g) plain, non-fat Greek Yogurt (Brian likes FAGE brand)

2 large egg yolks

1 packet gelatin powder

Sea salt to taste

***Optional:* garlic powder, onion powder, dill**

MACRONUTRIENTS PER SERVING: CALORIES: 208 FAT: 10 G CARBS: 3 G PROTEIN: 26 G

MAKES 1 SERVING

COOKING TIME:
10 MINUTES

YOKED
SCRAMBLED EGGS

Cooking the whites before adding in rich, creamy yolks really makes for the best scrambled eggs of your life.

1 tablespoon (15 g) butter

6 large eggs

Sea salt

1. Crack 6 eggs and separate whites and yolks.
2. Beat whites with sea salt.
3. Melt butter in pan on medium-high heat.
4. Scramble whites.
5. Add yolks and scramble for 10 seconds.
6. Remove from heat.

MACRONUTRIENTS PER SERVING: CALORIES: 522 FAT: 42 G CARBS: 0 G PROTEIN: 36 G

FISH

MAKES 4 SERVINGS

COOKING TIME:
20 MINUTES

AFRICAN FISH BALLS

Not 100% carnivore, but great way to eat nose-to-tail fish for people who don't normally like fish.

1 pound (454 g) whole fish (any variety), with skin and bones and all

3 tablespoons (45 g) natural, unsweetened peanut butter

½ (80 g) medium onion

1 garlic clove

Sea salt and pepper

Avocado oil spray

***Optional*: 1-2 peppers (jalapeno, habanero, serrano)**

1. Cut off fish head and tail and remove the main vertebrae from the meat and skin. It's okay if a few bones get left in, since they will get smashed up by the blender.
2. Blend the fish with the peanut butter, onion, garlic, salt & pepper, and optional spicy peppers. Start blender on low speed and gradually ramp up until you form a slurry.
3. Form golf ball or smaller-sized balls and set aside.
4. Heat cooking pan to medium-low heat and coat with a layer of avocado oil spray to prevent sticking.
5. Add fish balls to the pan and add water so that the balls are sitting in about a ½ inch of water
6. Cover pan and let cook for about 20 minutes or until balls start to brown and caramelize on the outside.

MACRONUTRIENTS PER SERVING: CALORIES: 239 FAT: 12 G CARBS: 5 G PROTEIN: 26 G

MAKES 1 SERVING

COOKING TIME:
15 MINUTES

AIR-FRIED SALMON

If you've got one of these nifty air fryers, you can make some delicious and easy salmon with it.

1 6-ounce (170 g) salmon fillet

1 teaspoon (5 g) sea salt

1. Season salmon fillet with sea salt.
2. Preheat air fryer for 5 minutes to at 210F (99C).
3. Set 1-2 sheets parchment paper in air fryer basket.
4. Cook at 390F (199C) for 7 minutes.
5. Serve!

MACRONUTRIENTS PER SERVING: CALORIES: 340 FAT: 20 G CARBS: 0 G PROTEIN: 61 G

MAKES 2 SERVINGS

COOKING TIME: 25 MINUTES

BACON-WRAPPED SALMON

This quick and easy meal is not only going to take care of your healthy fats and omega-3s, but the lemon wedges give it a perfect tang.

1. Preheat oven to 350F (177C).
2. Pat salmon fillets dry. Wrap 2 slices bacon around each fillet.
3. Place fillets on roasting tray and butter them. Bake for 15-20 minutes.
4. Serve with lemon wedges.

2 6-ounce (170 g) salmon fillets

4 slices bacon

1 tablespoon (15 g) butter

Lemon wedges

MACRONUTRIENTS PER SERVING: CALORIES: 471 FAT: 33 G CARBS: 0 G PROTEIN: 66 G

MAKES 1 SERVING

PREP TIME:
5 MINUTES

CARNIVORE "SALAD"

Super easy no-cook recipe you can throw together when you have the ingredients on hand.

1 4.4-ounce tin (125 g) of sardines, packed in water

1 3-ounce tin (85 g) of smoked oysters

4 ounces (113 g) crumbled U.S. Wellness Meats liverwurst or Braunschweiger

2 chopped large boiled eggs

Sea salt

1 scoop (20 g) Vital Proteins collagen peptides

Optional: Trader Joe's Everything but the Bagel Seasoning

1. Add drained sardines to bowl and "mash" with 1 scoop of collagen peptides until collagen dissolves into sardines.
2. Add remaining ingredients to bowl and season with sea salt to taste.

MACRONUTRIENTS PER SERVING: CALORIES: 807 FAT: 44 G CARBS: 8 G PROTEIN: 92 G

MAKES 1 SERVING

COOKING TIME: 20 MINUTES

CANNED SALMON EGG BAKE

This recipe uses staples from your kitchen—canned salmon, eggs, and butter. It's so easy, you don't even need dishes for this one. Just grab a fork and dig in.

1 6-ounce (170 g) can of salmon

½ tablespoon (7 g) butter

1 large egg

1. Preheat oven broiler or toaster oven.
2. Remove salmon from can and line inside of can with tin foil or parchment paper.
3. Add salmon back to can.
4. Top with a thin layer of butter, and crack egg on top.
5. Broil or toast can until egg white is crispy and yolk is slightly runny.

MACRONUTRIENTS PER SERVING: CALORIES: 427 FAT: 16 G CARBS: 0 G PROTEIN: 72 G

MAKES 1 SERVING

PREP TIME:
5 MINUTES

CLASSIC OYSTERS

You can't beat some fresh oysters with lemon juice and tabasco sauce. Give this a shot!

6 fresh oysters in shell

1 lemon

Tabasco sauce

1. Rinse fresh oysters.
2. Pop oysters open using thick knife or spoon.
3. Scoop oysters from bottom shell, ensuring no remaining shell fragments are attached.
4. Serve with squeezed lemon and tabasco sauce to taste.

MACRONUTRIENTS PER SERVING: CALORIES: 153 FAT: 2 G CARBS: 4 G PROTEIN: 6 G

MAKES 1 SERVING

COOKING TIME:
10 MINUTES

EASY SAUTÉED SALMON

Here's an easy salmon sauce recipe that will be done in no time. You'll be getting in some great protein, tons of micronutrients, and omega-3s to boot!

1 tablespoon (15 g) butter

1 6-ounce (170 g) Alaskan salmon fillet

½ teaspoon (2.5 g) sea salt

Black pepper

1. In a nonstick skillet, melt about 1 tablespoon (15 g) butter over medium-high heat and cook until foam subsides and turns deep gold in color, about 3 minutes.
2. Season the fillet with sea salt and pepper and add to pan, skin side up.
3. Cook without turning for about 6 minutes, until fish turns deep brown. Flip the fish and cook to taste until done (2 to 4 minutes longer). Enjoy!

MACRONUTRIENTS PER SERVING: CALORIES: 414 FAT: 30 G CARBS: 0 G PROTEIN: 36 G

MAKES 4 SERVINGS

PREP TIME:
30 MINUTES

FAUX CEVICHE SHRIMP

We're calling this faux ceviche because the shrimp is in fact already cooked. Cooked shrimp is easier to find and work with than raw shrimp.

1 pound (454 g) cooked small shrimp, peeled and deveined

Juice from 1 lime

1 tablespoon (10 g) minced red onion

¼ cup (15 g) minced, fresh cilantro

Sea salt

1. Place shrimp in a bowl with lime juice and let marinate for 20-30 minutes in the refrigerator.
2. Mix shrimp, onion, and cilantro together.
3. Salt to taste.

MACRONUTRIENTS PER SERVING: CALORIES: 138 FAT: 2 G CARBS: 1 G PROTEIN: 25 G

MAKES 1 SERVING

COOKING TIME:
10 MINUTES

LOBSTER OMELET

Changing up this breakfast classic with some delicious lobster!

2 large eggs

Sea salt

2 tablespoons (3 g) mixed fresh herbs

1 ounce (28 g) cheese, for grating

1 cup (100 g) lobster meat

1 tablespoon (15 g) butter

1. Crack two eggs in bowl. Add sea salt and mixed herbs. Grate cheese into egg mixture. Whisk together. Add lobster meat.
2. Melt butter in medium-low heat pan. Add lobster omelet mixture. Cover with lid. Let cook until outsides are firm. Flip omelet once.
3. Enjoy!

MACRONUTRIENTS PER SERVING: CALORIES: 493 FAT: 33 G CARBS: 7 G PROTEIN: 47 G

MAKES 2 SERVINGS

PREP TIME:
10 MINUTES

OMEGA BUTTER

This is a great make-ahead superfood meal for traveling, backpacking, camping, etc., that keeps you cognitively lit up and energized when sitting down for a meal any time soon isn't possible.

2 4.4-ounce (125 g) tins of sardines, packed in water

2 ounces (57 g) macadamia nuts

2 tablespoons (30 g) coconut or MCT Oil

Sea salt to taste

1. Combine all ingredients except for sea salt in a food processor or high-speed blender.
2. Blend until smooth.
3. Add sea salt to taste.
4. Store in the freezer. (This can also be stored in reusable food pouches in the refrigerator and then taken on the go.)

MACRONUTRIENTS PER SERVING: CALORIES: 507 FAT: 40 G CARBS: 4 G PROTEIN: 35 G

MAKES 2 SERVINGS

COOKING TIME:
20 MINUTES

PARMESAN CRUSTED COD

Parmesan crusted anything is great—try this!

1 cup (100 g) grated parmesan cheese

1 teaspoon (5 g) sea salt

1 teaspoon (5 g) paprika

1 tablespoon (15 g) melted butter

2 6-ounce (170 g) cod fillets

1. Preheat oven to 400F (204C).
2. Line a baking sheet with parchment paper.
3. Mix the parmesan, paprika, and sea salt. Drizzle the melted butter over the cod fillets and then mix the fillets in the parmesan spice mixture. Press the cheese and spices into the cod fillets.
4. Transfer to the baking sheet. Top the cod fillets with leftover parmesan cheese.
5. Bake 10-15 minutes, enjoy!

MACRONUTRIENTS PER SERVING: CALORIES: 429 FAT: 25 G CARBS: 1 G PROTEIN: 54 G

MAKES 4 SERVINGS

COOKING TIME:
10 MINUTES

PRESTO PESTO SCALLOPS

This seems like a gourmet meal, but the whole thing can be made in 10 minutes or so. This can also be used as an appetizer for when you are invited to a party and asked to bring appetizers. Just get some toothpicks and everyone can have a scallop.

1 pound (454 g) scallops (find frozen at Trader Joes or big box store, or fresh at a fish market or quality grocer. You can use large or baby scallops)—large recommended

1 bunch, or small plastic container (.66 ounce/18 g) fresh basil

½ cup (70 g) pine nuts

⅓ cup (80 ml) extra-virgin domestic olive oil

1 tablespoon (15 ml) lemon juice

1 tablespoon (15 g) butter

Assorted spices

***Optional*: sun-dried tomatoes, ½ medium (80 g) onion, pureed**

Note: *If you are using baby scallops, continually churn the scallops instead of following the big scallop directions.*

1. Puree the basil and pine nuts.
2. Add olive oil, gradually, as you puree to achieve the desired consistency of store-bought pestos made with disgusting canola oil. Shame on the otherwise super cool Costco Kirkland brand!
3. Add lemon juice, desired spices, and any optional ingredients. Right now, the clock is at probably two minutes.
4. Rinse the scallops in warm water and make sure there is no residual ice.
5. Heat the butter in a cast-iron skillet on medium-high. When the butter is melted, carefully place the scallops into the skillet so each has a clean application of one side to the bottom of the skillet.
6. After around 90 seconds, flip each scallop individually to cook the other side. The end goal is to have a nice browning of the sides and a soft middle. Since you eat scallops raw at the sushi bar, please err on the undercooked side rather than turning your expensive scallops into rubber canine chew toys.
7. After cooking the second side, throw the scallops into the pesto mixture and stir well. This is best served immediately while the scallops are warm.

MACRONUTRIENTS PER SERVING: CALORIES: 419 FAT: 33 G CARBS: 12 G PROTEIN: 25 G

MAKES 6 SERVINGS

COOKING TIME: 10 MINUTES

SALMON FETA BURGERS

Salmon and feta are simply a great combo. If you've got a burger hankering and want your omega-3 fix, whip these up!

1 pound (454 g) salmon

2 ounces (57 g) feta

1 ½ tablespoons (21 ml) lemon juice

Black pepper to taste

1. Slice the salmon into small cubes and mash together with hands to create small chunks. Add to large mixing bowl. Add the crumbled feta, lemon juice, and black pepper.
2. Mix together with hands until the cheese and salmon are mixed well together.
3. Form 6 patties.
4. Grill or cook on the skillet for 3 minutes per side until burgers are cooked throughout.
5. Enjoy!

MACRONUTRIENTS PER SERVING: CALORIES: 108 FAT: 7 G CARBS: 1 G PROTEIN: 16 G

MAKES 1 SERVING

COOKING TIME: 5 MINUTES

SARDINES 'N SUN-DRIED

It's recipes like this that make life worth living and this book worth writing. If you've been working hard all morning and are ready for a short break, or you're home late and not into preparing a gourmet dinner, this colorful and creative meal can be made in a few minutes.

2 4.4-ounce (125 g) tins of sardines packed, in olive oil

3 tablespoons (21 g) sun-dried tomatoes (make sure your brand isn't swimming in bad oils)

1 ounce (28 g) walnuts

1. Heat a skillet with a little butter and add the sardines and sun-dried tomatoes. Stir fry.
2. Once cooked, crush the walnuts in your hand and sprinkle on top. A tablespoon (15 g) of Primal Kitchen Chipotle Lime Mayo or Green Goddess Dressing works well here too.

MACRONUTRIENTS PER SERVING: CALORIES: 430 FAT: 26 G CARBS: 14 G PROTEIN: 35 G

MAKES 4 SERVINGS

COOKING TIME: 20 MINUTES

SHEET PAN SHRIMP BOIL

Old Bay Seasoning really makes this dish outstanding. Try to get the highest quality shrimp you can find, and check for simple ingredients in the sausages, avoiding fillers and preservatives.

¼ cup (60 g) butter, melted

3 cloves minced garlic

1 tablespoon (7 g) Old Bay Seasoning

1 pound (454 g) medium shrimp, peeled and deveined

12 ounces (342 g) smoked andouille sausage

1 lemon

1. Preheat oven to 400F (204 C).
2. Lightly oil baking sheet.
3. In a small bowl, combine butter, garlic and Old Bay Seasoning.
4. Cut sausage into thin pieces.
5. Place shrimp and sausage on baking sheet in single layer.
6. Pour butter mixture over the sheet, tossing lightly to combine.
7. Bake for about 15 minutes, or until the shrimp is opaque.
8. Serve with lemon wedges.

MACRONUTRIENTS PER SERVING: CALORIES: 588 FAT: 44 G CARBS: 9 G PROTEIN: 35 G

MAKES 4 SERVINGS

PREP TIME:
1 HOUR

SIMPLE CEVICHE

This is perfect for a Summer night out on the patio and is sure to be a crowd pleaser at your next get together. We bet most people won't know that they are eating carnivore when you serve them this dish.

1 pound (454 g) any fresh, white, lean fish fillet

3 limes

2 lemons

½ medium (80 g) red onion

¼ cup (15 g) chopped cilantro

Sea salt to taste

1. Slice fish into small, bite-sized pieces.
2. Zest the lemon and lime, and grate them fine using a microplane grater.
3. Juice the limes and lemons.
4. Chop the onion.
5. Add all ingredients except for cilantro to a bowl and marinate for 1 hour.
6. Add chopped cilantro, salt to taste, and serve cold.

MACRONUTRIENTS PER SERVING: CALORIES: 209 FAT: 9 G CARBS: 4 G PROTEIN: 28 G

MAKES 2 SERVINGS

COOKING TIME:
10 MINUTES

STEAK AND OYSTERS

Shewfelt's steak and oysters pack a major nutritional punch and they taste amazing. They may even confer some fringe benefits (aphrodisiac anyone?). But enough about that...let's get cooking.

1 New York strip steak

1 3-ounce (85 g) tin of oysters, packed in olive oil

Himalayan pink salt

Black pepper

Primal Kitchen Steak Sauce

1. Heat the grill to high. Liberally salt the steak with Himalayan pink salt and black pepper.
2. Place the steak on the grill for 4 to 5 minutes or until it starts to brown and is slightly charred.
3. Open the tin of oysters and carefully place them on the grill near the steak.
4. Flip the steak and continue to grill for 3-5 minutes.
5. Flip the oysters after 1 minute and grill for 1 more minute.
6. Serve immediately with Primal Kitchen Steak Sauce.

MACRONUTRIENTS PER SERVING: CALORIES: 379 FAT: 26 G CARBS: 6 G PROTEIN: 28 G

MAKES 4 SERVINGS

COOKING TIME:
15 MINUTES

THE NOSE-TO-TAIL MEAL MUSCLE BOWL

Still think this diet is burgers and bacon? Well it is...but not just burgers and bacon. Try this meal out and see if you don't feel like you're 18 again. The incredible nutrient density afforded you by these nutrient-rich foods will leave you feeling amazing. Have this meal once a week or every few weeks just to make sure your nutrients are all topped up!

6 medium oysters

1 pound (454 g) Organ Meat Burger from NoseToTail.org

2 pastured large eggs

1 4.4-ounce (125 g) tin of sardines, packed in water

1 tablespoon (15 g) smelt or salmon roe

15 chicken hearts

1 tablespoon (15 g) beef tallow

Pink salt

Black pepper

Tabasco sauce

Lime juice

1. Heat pan on medium-high heat and melt 1 tablespoon (15 g) of beef tallow. Form the organ meat burger into two beef patties. Season generously with pink salt and black pepper.
2. When fat is melted, reduce heat to medium-low and place the burger patties on the pan. Let cook for 5 minutes before flipping it and letting cook for another 5 minutes.
3. Once the burger patties have cooked, plate them and tent with foil to preserve heat. Crack two pastured eggs in the same pan and let the egg whites harden. Season with black pepper and sea salt.
4. Flip the eggs after 3-5 minutes. Let cook for another 2 minutes. Plate the eggs.
5. Place the chicken hearts in the pan and season with salt. Let cook for 3-5 minutes before plating.
6. Add 6 fresh oysters to plate and season with tabasco sauce and lime juice.
7. Add salmon or smelt roe to plate. Add sardines to plate.

MACRONUTRIENTS PER SERVING: CALORIES: 224 FAT: 12 G CARBS: 4 G PROTEIN: 24 G

MAKES 2 SERVINGS

COOKING TIME:
10 MINUTES

TUNA PATTIES

Adding collagen to this recipe makes these tuna patties even more nutritious. Make sure you always have some in your pantry and discover all the ways to sneak it into meals.

1 large egg

2 5-ounce (142 g) cans of tuna

2 tablespoons (18 g) unflavored hydrolysate collagen

1 tablespoon (15 ml) water

1 tablespoon (15 g) yellow mustard

Sea salt

1 tablespoon (15 g) beef tallow

***Optional:* lemon**

1. Mix egg with drained tuna, collagen, water, mustard, sea salt, and if desired, other seasonings.
2. Form patties and let chill in the fridge for 1 hour.
3. Heat tallow in pan on medium-high heat.
4. Cook 3-4 minutes per side, until brown on both sides.
5. Garnish with lemon slices.

MACRONUTRIENTS PER SERVING: CALORIES: 353 FAT: 18 G CARBS: 1 G PROTEIN: 41 G

MAKES 1 SERVING

COOKING TIME: 15 MINUTES

VENISON AND SALMON ROE

Alright, enough steak and eggs. Let's get real primal here. Ancient man wasn't just hunting down cows all day...we were hunting down deer as well! Combine that with some salmon roe and you've got a serious nutritional-powerhouse meal.

½ pound (198 g) wild venison

2 ounces (57 g) red salmon roe

2 teaspoons (10 g) beef tallow

1. Set heat to medium. Melt 2 teaspoons (10 g) beef tallow on skillet.
2. Cook wild venison on skillet, seasoning each side with salt, 5 minutes per side.
3. Plate and add salmon roe to plate. Enjoy!

MACRONUTRIENTS PER SERVING: CALORIES: 611 FAT: 28 G CARBS: 0 G PROTEIN: 89 G

MEAT

MAKES 4 SERVINGS

COOKING TIME:
30 MINUTES

80/20 MEATBALLS

Here's a great way for people who don't like the taste of liver to sneak some liver into their carnivore diet.

13 ounces (370 g) ground beef or steak

3 ounces (85 g) beef liver

¼ medium (40 g) onion

Sea salt

***Optional:* any additional seasonings**

1. Preheat oven to 350F (177C).
2. Add beef, liver, onion, and sea salt (plus any additional seasoning) to food processor.
3. Combine on low until fully blended together.
4. Place a cooling rack over a sheet pan.
5. Scoop out 8 balls and place on rack.
6. Bake for 20-30 minutes.

1 SERVING = 2 MEATBALLS
MACRONUTRIENTS PER SERVING: CALORIES: 219 FAT: 13 G CARBS: 2 G PROTEIN: 24 G

MAKES 4 SERVINGS

COOKING TIME:
15 MINUTES

B-MAC'S
GROUND BEEF

Ground beef will likely become a staple for you with this way of eating. Canned tomato paste is a convenient and economical addition that helps hide the taste of the added liver, and it carries very little downsides. Most people who are sensitive to tomatoes are aggravated by the peel and seeds and those things are removed in the processing. Sometimes a little processing isn't such a bad thing.

1 pound (454 g) 93/7 ground beef

½ of a 6-ounce (170 g) can of tomato paste

1 frozen liver cube

2 tablespoons (18 g) unflavored hydrolysate gelatin

Sea salt

1. Flatten out ground beef in casti-iron pan and heat to medium-high.
2. Stir as pan starts to heat up to prevent sticking.
3. Once ground beef starts to brown, add in 1 frozen liver cube (made ahead by running liver through food processor and freezing in ice cube tray).
4. At some point in the cooking time, ground beef will give off a lot of water. At this time, add in the gelatin and stir.
5. As water starts to evaporate, add in tomato paste and stir.
6. Cook until excess liquid evaporates. Salt to taste.

MACRONUTRIENTS PER SERVING: CALORIES: 429 FAT: 17 G CARBS: 9 G PROTEIN: 58 G

MAKES 8 SERVINGS

COOKING TIME:
40 MINUTES

BACON-WRAPPED MEATBALLS

Shewfelt says, "Okay you've been eating steaks and burgers on repeat—there has to be more to the carnivore diet?! Well not really, but you can get adventurous and try this delicious meatball recipe. Note: It includes pork and some non-carnivore seasonings, so if you don't tolerate seasonings well, best to stick to pink salt."

1 pound (454 g) ground pork

1 pound (454 g) ground beef

1 large egg, beaten

¼ cup (25 g) grated parmesan

Italian seasonings

Garlic powder

Himalayan pink salt

Black pepper

Primal Kitchen Classic BBQ Sauce

16-18 bacon slices cut in half

1. Preheat the oven to 350F (177C).
2. Put ground pork and ground beef in bowl. Add beaten egg. Then add parmesan, Italian seasonings, garlic, pink salt, and black pepper in bowl. Mix ingredients together well.
3. Line a baking sheet with foil and place a baking rack on top of the sheet.
4. Form the meat into meatballs. Wrap the meat in bacon strips and place the bacon-wrapped meatballs on the rack.
5. Bake for 15 minutes
6. Apply the Primal Kitchen barbecue sauce.
7. Bake for another 15 minutes.
8. Serve immediately.

MACRONUTRIENTS PER SERVING: CALORIES: 345 FAT: 26 G CARBS: 1 G PROTEIN: 27 G

CLASSIC
ORGANIC
NO ADDED SUGAR
SOY FREE

ORGANIC
BEEF LIVER
WHOLE
INGREDIENTS:

MAKES 20 PATTIES

COOKING TIME: 30 MINUTES

BADASS BURGER INFUSION

Start with some exceptionally high-quality ground meat, and infuse with this creative blend to make a softer, more delicious burger. Ground buffalo is the bomb and a refreshing upgrade from the typical ground beef offerings. Visit WildIdeaBuffalo.com to learn about these amazing free-range, grass-fed, humanely-harvested animals that represent one of the best choices in premium beef. Ground lamb is also awesome; choose New Zealand varieties, because all New Zealand lamb is grass-fed. Japanese style wagyu beef is also superior.

If you are using ground beef, go grass-fed or at least organic or go home. It's time to reject conventional ground beef. Those cattle are fed chemical-laden grains (that ruin their fatty acid profile) and even candy (with the wrappers still on) while fattening up like crazy for a traumatic slaughter. *Fact:* Forty million cattle are slaughtered each year in filthy slaughterhouses and packing houses. Only 60,000 buffalo are humanely harvested each year.

4 pounds (1820 g) ground buffalo, lamb, wagyu, or grass-fed beef

1 pound (454 g) liver

1 medium (160 g) red onion

2 cups (250 g) walnuts, pecans, or almonds

2 pastured eggs

3 tablespoons (21 g) sun-dried tomatoes (make sure your brand don't got nasty industrial seed oil in the jar)

2 tablespoons (30 g) plain, full-fat yogurt

¼ cup (60 ml) fresh or bottled lemon juice

2 cups (134 g) fresh organic kale

Spices: generous applications of mineral salt and mixed spices

Melted cheese to add onto the patties just before they're done

1 medium (150 g) avocado for topping the finished patties

1. Wash your hands. Why do we even have to remind you? Should be obvious.
2. Use a big Cuisinart or multiple uses of small Ninja to puree all the ingredients in this exact order: whatever you want first, followed by whatever you want next, etc., till they are in there and mixed up.
3. Throw everything into large mixing bowl and shape into patties. If you find your mixture isn't forming patties easily, or if your patties don't hold their form once you start cooking them, just mince it all up in the skillet, it will still taste like the best thing, ever.
4. Melt 2 tablespoons (30 g) of butter on your huge-ass heavy-duty cast-iron skillet, heated to medium-high.
5. Cook the patties on medium-high with the skillet covered. Realize these will be softer than straight ground meat. It's okay to cut into one to make sure the interior is cooked completely. Ideally you will bite into a browned, slightly crunchy exterior and a delicious soft interior which will take between 4-6 minutes per side. Cook the patties in batches since you'll be making a lot and enjoying leftovers. Serve with sliced avocado on top. Realize that with a meal this good, you never need a bun, and may never eat a chemically flavored fast food burger again.

MACRONUTRIENTS PER SERVING: CALORIES: 363 FAT: 22 G CARBS: 4 G PROTEIN: 24 G

Emerging science is suggesting that avocados are so delicious they might be reclassified as a small mammal soon.

MAKES 5 SERVINGS

COOKING TIME:
2 HOURS
AND 15 MINUTES

BBQ PORK RIBS

This is one to be shared with the family or friends. Pork ribs are a cost-effective option on a carnivore diet—and damn good!

6 pounds (2724 g) baby back pork ribs

Sea salt

Primal Kitchen Golden BBQ Sauce

1. Preheat oven to 275F (135C).
2. Remove membrane from the back of the ribs.
3. Season the ribs generously with sea salt on both sides.
4. Completely wrap the ribs in foil and close up. Place on baking sheet.
5. Bake for 2 hours. Remove from oven and drain the juices. Brush BBQ sauce on the ribs—then broil for another 5 minutes.
6. Remove ribs and plate. Enjoy!

MACRONUTRIENTS PER SERVING: CALORIES: 584 FAT: 41 G CARBS: 3 G PROTEIN: 46 G

MAKES 8 SERVINGS

COOKING TIME: 4-10 HOURS, DEPENDING ON SLOW-COOKER SETTING

BEEF SHORT RIBS

Craving some good, fatty ribs? We got you! We're gonna make this one delicious without the sugary sauces most restaurants use.

4 pounds (1816 g) bone-in beef short ribs

2 tablespoons (30 g) butter

1 cup (240 ml) bone broth

2 tablespoons (30 ml) Worcestershire sauce

Sea salt

Pepper

1. Heat butter in large skillet over medium-high heat.
2. Season short ribs with salt and pepper, then place onto hot skillet and brown each side.
3. Add beef broth to slow cooker and place short ribs into cooker.
4. Cover and cook on low heat for 8-10 hours (juicier, more tender) or on high heat for 4-6 hours.
5. Plate and serve with Worcestershire sauce and salt to taste!

MACRONUTRIENTS PER SERVING: CALORIES: 403 FAT: 23 G CARBS: 1 G PROTEIN: 48 G

MAKES 8 SERVINGS

COOKING TIME:
15 MINUTES

BLUE CHEESE BUFFALO BURGER

This one takes the cake (...or steak?) for my absolute favorite carnivore meal. Blue cheese and buffalo—you can't go wrong.

2 pounds (908 g) ground bison

2 teaspoons (10 g) Himalayan pink salt

Black pepper

½ (230 g) cup crumbled blue cheese

1. Season ground buffalo with pink salt and pepper. Form the ground bison into 6-8 balls.
2. Create a hole in each ball and press a tablespoon (15 g) of blue cheese into the hole. Seal the meat around the cheese. Press each ball into patties.
3. Pan-fry the burgers on medium heat for 4-6 minutes each side. Serve and enjoy!

MACRONUTRIENTS PER SERVING: CALORIES: 303 FAT: 23 G CARBS: 1 G PROTEIN: 24 G

MAKES 2 SERVINGS

TOTAL TIME:
15 MINUTES

BRIAN'S 10-MINUTE SIRLOIN STEAK

Sirloin is such a great cut of steak. Buy the highest quality you can and keep it in your freezer so that you can grill up this simple recipe any time you like. Experiment with different salts, such as Real Salt or Himalayan pink salt.

1 pound (454 g) top sirloin steak

Sea salt

Optional:
Serve with Primal Kitchen BBQ or Steak Sauce.

1. Preheat grill (keeping it covered).
2. Cut thick cut steaks into thin ones by slicing thickness in half.
3. Season with sea salt.
4. When grill temp reaches higher than 450F (232C), add steaks to top rack (elevated above the grill).
5. Cook 3 minutes per side, keeping grill closed.
6. Flip steaks, then move to lower grill level.
7. Close grill and let cook for 2 more minutes per side.
8. Let rest for 5 minutes.
9. Slice down the middle (the long way) and then across into bite-sized strips.

MACRONUTRIENTS PER SERVING: CALORIES: 456 FAT: 29 G CARBS: 0 G PROTEIN: 45 G

MAKES 1 SERVING

COOKING TIME:
20 MINUTES

CARNIVORE GOURMET BURGERS

Who needs flimsy hamburger buns that only contribute to spiked insulin when you've got two insanely delicious beef patties and creamy, melted cheddar cheese? Served with a fried egg and bacon, this recipe is truly a delicacy.

1 large egg

1 ounce (28 g) cheddar cheese

2 4-ounce (113 g) burger patties

2 slices bacon

1 tablespoon (15 g) butter

Sea salt

1. Season beef patties with salt. Melt 1 tablespoon (15 g) butter on medium heat in a cast-iron skillet. Slap the beef patties on the cast iron. Let cook for 5 minutes per side.
2. In a separate pan, set heat to medium and cook bacon until crispy. Set bacon aside and fry 1 egg in bacon grease for 2-3 minutes. Season egg with sea salt.
3. Place 1 ounce (28 g) of cheese in between burger patties. Top the burger patties with fried egg and bacon slices. Enjoy!

Optional:
Cook egg so it's runny for extra decadence.

MACRONUTRIENTS PER SERVING: CALORIES: 976 FAT: 86 G CARBS: 1 G PROTEIN: 47 G

MAKES 4 SERVINGS

COOKING TIME:
20 MINUTES

CARNIVORE
MUSCLE BOWL

The Muscle Bowl is Shewfelt's personal favorite simple and delicious carnivore meal. "It ain't pretty...but it's damn good. It's quick, simple, and will keep you lean...all while being absolutely delicious. Eat up! No anti-nutrients here," he explains.

1 pound (454 g) ground beef

4 large eggs

1 cup (55 g) canned salmon or 1 4.4 ounce-tin (125 g) of sardines

⅓ cup (35 g) shredded cheese

Himalayan pink salt

1. Heat a medium-sized pan to medium heat. Add 1 pound (454 g) of ground beef and use a spatula to separate it and spread it out evenly across the pan. Add salmon or sardines.

2. Generously add Himalayan pink salt. Put a lid on the pan and turn to medium-low for 5-7 minutes, occasionally using spatula to move the ground beef around and cook evenly.

3. Add 4 whole eggs. Add more pink salt. Stir the eggs into the beef. As the egg begins to set on the bottom, use the spatula to flip it in the pan and swirl the liquid egg portions around to evenly cook.

4. When the beef and egg mixture is set, slide the entire mixture into a straining bowl over the sink. Allow the excess fat and liquid to drain into the sink. Then put the beef-egg-fish mixture back into the pan.

5. Slide the food onto a plate using a spatula and add shredded cheese on top. Serve immediately.

MACRONUTRIENTS PER SERVING: CALORIES: 372 FAT: 24 G CARBS: 1 G PROTEIN: 39 G

MAKES 4 SERVINGS

COOKING TIME:
20 MINUTES

DR. CATE'S SUPER *TESTOSTERONE BOOSTING* STEW

While many foods have a scientifically validated testosterone boosting effect, Cool Dudes should never discount the importance of the placebo effect, which is believed to represent 38 percent of all healing. In Dr. Bruce Lipton's *Biology of Belief*, he describes the profound impact your thoughts can have on your physiology. Each cell in your body has perception switches that process information from the environment, including thoughts and direct accordant genetic and hormonal processes. If you miss your flight and get pissed, stress hormones will flood your bloodstream. If you laugh, smile, and cry tears of joy while reading a great new cookbook, mood elevating hormones like serotonin and dopamine flood the bloodstream. If you think of yourself a brave, bold, confident manly man with high testosterone levels, you can actually manifest these thoughts into reality. As Lipton asserts, "If the perception in your mind is reflected in the chemistry of your body, and if your nervous system reads and interprets the environment and then controls the blood's chemistry, then you can literally change the fate of your cells by altering your thoughts."

1. Peel and chop the onion and tomato and set aside.
2. In a skillet on medium heat, sear each side of the sliced meat for 1 minute, or until browned.
3. Add the chopped onion, chopped tomato, tomato paste, and water and reduce to a simmer until the meat is tender and the stew juices have thickened, about 15 minutes.
4. Season with sea salt to taste.

1 pound (454 g) stew meat, sliced in thick chunks

1 medium (160 g) onion

1 medium (123 g) tomato

1 6-ounce (150 g) can of tomato paste

2 cups (480 ml) water

Sea salt

MACRONUTRIENTS PER SERVING: CALORIES: 248 FAT: 12 G CARBS: 13 G PROTEIN: 22 G

MAKES 1 SERVING

COOKING TIME:
10 MINUTES

EXPRESS
STEAK AND EGGS

Here's a recipe for steak and eggs for when you're in a hurry. Microwaved eggs are not as gross as you'd think and are actually pretty decent using a bit of bone broth and a bit of practice.

4 ounces (113 g) top sirloin or other lean steak

2 large eggs

Sea salt

2 tablespoons (30 g) boxed bone broth

***Optional:* beef tallow**

1. Heat grill pan or cast-iron skillet on medium-high heat. (Use beef tallow if needed.)
2. If steaks are thick, cut them down the middle to make them less than an inch thick. Season with sea salt.
3. When pan is hot and almost smoking, add steaks and cook for 3-4 minutes per side.
4. While steaks are cooking, add 2 eggs and 2 tablespoons (30 g) boxed bone broth to a mug and whisk with a fork.
5. Microwave mug for 45 seconds.
6. Stir eggs, and microwave for another 45 seconds.
7. Let steak rest a minute or two and serve with eggs.

MACRONUTRIENTS PER SERVING: CALORIES: 406 FAT: 15 G CARBS: 5 G PROTEIN: 60 G

MAKES 8 SERVINGS

COOKING TIME:
5-8 HOURS

GRASS-FED CHUCK ROAST

It literally doesn't get any easier than this. If you don't have a Crock-Pot or other slow cooker, you can always grab one at the store for $20 or $30.

2 pounds (908 g) chuck roast

Sea salt

1. Season chuck roast with sea salt on each side.
2. Set to low heat in Crock-Pot and let cook for 5-8 hours.
3. Enjoy!

MACRONUTRIENTS PER SERVING: CALORIES: 253 FAT: 18 G CARBS: 0 G PROTEIN: 28 G

MAKES 1 SERVING

COOKING TIME:
10 MINUTES

HAM BREAKFAST TACOS

Why haven't breakfast tacos been served like this all along? Ham slices are sturdy and work so well to hold scrambled eggs and hot sauce, making carnivore even easier than you thought.

5 large eggs

1 tablespoon (15 g) beef tallow

Sea salt

4 slices deli ham

***Optional*: Tapatio or Cholula Hot Sauce**

1. Heat frying pan on medium heat.
2. Whisk eggs in a bowl using a fork.
3. Add sea salt.
4. Melt tallow in frying pan.
5. Add eggs to pan and scramble.
6. When eggs are scrambled, remove from pan and set aside.
7. Add ham slices to pan and brown slightly.
8. Remove ham from pan and dry with a paper towel.
9. Serve scrambled eggs inside of ham, using the slices like tortillas.
10. Garnish with hot sauce.

MACRONUTRIENTS PER SERVING: CALORIES: 540 FAT: 42 G CARBS: 0 G PROTEIN: 40 G

MAKES 1 SERVING

COOKING TIME:
15 MINUTES

KETO BREATH SALAD

If this doesn't get you blowing acetone, we don't know what will.

2 cups (200 g) shredded cabbage

2 tablespoons (30 ml) Pure C8 MCT Oil

1 tablespoon (15 g) spicy brown mustard

1 large (100 g) Kiolbassa sausage

Seasonings/spices

***Optional*: chicharrones or crunchy cheese snack for crouton-like crunch**

1. On a grill, cook 1 large (100 g) Kiolbassa sausage. If you don't have a grill, cook it in a stovetop cast-iron pan in a thin layer of water.
2. While the sausage is cooking, cut up roughly 2 cups (200 g) of cabbage thinly into shreds.
3. In a large mixing bowl, mix cabbage with 2 tablespoons (30 ml) of MCT oil, a large squirt of mustard, and a bit of spices and seasoning. Stir until cabbage starts to soften.
4. When the sausage is fully cooked, chop up and add to the mixing bowl with either chicharrones or crunchy cheese "croutons."

MACRONUTRIENTS PER SERVING: CALORIES: 429 FAT: 42 G CARBS: 8 G PROTEIN: 7 G

MAKES 4 SERVINGS

COOKING TIME:
30 MINUTES

LAMB "DONUTS" WITH YOGURT MINT SAUCE

Lamb paired with Greek yogurt and mint is really, really tasty. It's even easier to form these into "donuts" by baking them in a bundt pan, which are found in the baking section at most stores.

"Donuts"

1 pound (454 g) ground lamb

1 tablespoon (9 g) unflavored hydrolysate gelatin

Sea salt

Black pepper

Sauce

1 cup (240 g) plain, non-fat Greek yogurt

1 clove minced garlic

2 tablespoons (3 g) chopped fresh mint

½ tablespoon (7 ml) lemon juice

½ tablespoon (7 g) sea salt

1. Preheat oven to 350F (177C).
2. Mix gelatin with ground lamb and form 4 "donuts."
3. Place on a cooling rack over a baking sheet and bake for about 20-30 minutes until brown and outside is firm.
4. Mix yogurt, garlic, mint, lemon juice, and sea salt in a small bowl.
5. Allow lamb to cool and serve. Top or dip with yogurt sauce.

MACRONUTRIENTS PER SERVING: CALORIES: 356 FAT: 27 G CARBS: 3 G PROTEIN: 26 G

MAKES 5 SERVINGS

COOKING TIME: 20 MINUTES

MAMA SHEWFELT'S CARNIVORE BUFFET

This meal was simply inspired by an amazing meal the General of the Shewfelt Household (Will's dear mother) made. Will told her about the carnivore diet, and she said "Don't worry about it. I gotcha"—or something to that effect. And the rest was history. Mama Shewfelt…this one's for you!

1 ½ pounds (681 g) ribeye steak

1 pound (454 g) peeled, thawed, frozen, bagged shrimp

1 pound (454 g) chile lime sausage

5 soft-boiled large eggs

1 teaspoon (5 g) black pepper

Himalayan pink salt

1 teaspoon (5 g) Caribeque Jamaican Jerk seasoning

1. Set pan to medium-high heat. Season ribeye steak on both sides with black pepper and Jamaican jerk seasoning. Sear both sides of steak in pan for 2-3 minutes each side with lid on. Tent with foil to preserve heat.
2. Reduce heat to medium. Place thawed shrimp in same pan and toss for 2 minutes, with lid on. Set shrimp aside.
3. Bring heat to medium-high. Place sausages in same pan and let sauté for 5-6 minutes, turning sausages every 1-2 minutes. After 5-6 minutes, slice sausage to check if fully cooked. If not, continue cooking until ready. Set sausage aside.
4. Fill pot with water enough to cover five eggs and bring to a boil. Then place eggs in boiling water and let boil for 5 minutes. Then immediately remove eggs with tongs and place eggs in cold water. Peel eggs under cold running water. Cut in half and sprinkle with salt and pepper.
5. Devour with gusto. Bon appetit!

MACRONUTRIENTS PER SERVING: CALORIES: 611 FAT: 35 G CARBS: 3 G PROTEIN: 69 G

MAKES 3 SERVINGS

COOKING TIME: 30 MINUTES

CHEESY BACON MEATLOAF

"Oh, I'm so tired of eating delicious steak every night...this diet is so hard." Quit your complaining and try this! Your taste buds will cry tears of joy. And your fat cells will cry tears of agony.

1 large egg

1 pound (454 g) ground beef

1 cup (30 g) pork rind crumbs

1 tablespoon (15 ml) Primal Kitchen Italian Vinaigrette

½ cup (62 g) shredded cheese

½ cup (113 g) bacon crumbles

3 tablespoons (45 g) Primal Kitchen Spicy Ketchup

1. Mix ground beef, eggs, pork rind crumbs, vinaigrette, shredded cheese, and bacon crumbles in a bowl.
2. Form 3 meat loafs. Place each on baking tray.
3. Top with Primal Kitchen Spicy Ketchup, more shredded cheese, and some more bacon crumbles.
4. Cook for 20 minutes at 350F (177C). Cooking time may vary!

MACRONUTRIENTS PER SERVING: CALORIES: 527 FAT: 35 G CARBS: 3 G PROTEIN: 46 G

MAKES 2 SERVINGS

COOKING TIME:
20 MINUTES

Here's another creative carnivore recipe that will get you carnivore shredded. Shewfelt explains to dudes, "Steaks can drive your grocery bill up, and plain burgers can get old real fast—so try this to spice up an old classic."

MUSTARD
BACON BURGERS

1 pound (454 g) ground beef

4 ounces (113 g) bacon, diced

Himalayan pink salt

Black pepper

4 teaspoons (20 g) yellow mustard

1. Heat a pan to medium-high and cook bacon in the pan until crispy. Leave the bacon grease in the pan and put the bacon bits into a bowl with the ground beef. Season with pink salt and black pepper and mix together.
2. Form the ground beef into 4 burger patties.
3. Sear the burgers in the pan on high heat. Cook for 2 minutes, then flip the patties and cook for 2 more minutes.
4. Once cooked, apply 1 teaspoon (5 g) of mustard to each of the burger patties—flip the patties and let them sear in the mustard for 30 seconds. Serve immediately.

MACRONUTRIENTS PER SERVING: CALORIES: 502 FAT: 34 G CARBS: 1 G PROTEIN: 48 G

Nut Butter Ground Beef is delicious enough to serve to your favorite New York Times bestselling author and ancestral health movement icon... especially if you're taking over his kitchen...

MAKES 4 SERVINGS

COOKING TIME:
10 MINUTES

NUT BUTTER GROUND BEEF

Macadamia and cashew nut butter are solid choices for those looking to minimize oxalates.

1 pound (454 g) lean ground beef

2 tablespoons (30 g) macadamia or cashew butter

2 scoops (20 g) Vital Proteins Collagen Peptides

1. Heat saucepan or skillet on medium-high heat.
2. Brown ground beef.
3. Once ground beef is browned, mix in nut butter.
4. Mix in collagen peptides, then remove from heat and serve.

MACRONUTRIENTS PER SERVING: CALORIES: 295 FAT: 21 G CARBS: 1 G PROTEIN: 27 G

MAKES 3 SERVINGS

COOKING TIME:
10 MINUTES
PLUS SOAKING TIME
FOR CASHEWS

POLIQUIN'S MEAT & NUT BREAKFAST

This recipe is in honor of strength coach legend Charles Poliquin. Cashews are creamy and a little sweet and maybe not surprisingly good in ground beef. Soak them overnight if you can. But if you don't have that much time, a few hours will work in a pinch.

¾ pound (342 g) 93/7 ground beef or ground bison

1 ½ ounces (43 g) raw cashews or macadamia nuts

2 scoops (20 g) Vital Protein Collagen Peptides

1 tablespoon (15 g) boxed bone broth

Sea salt

1. Before you go to bed, place cashews in a cup of water and soak overnight in the fridge.
2. Wake up and heat pan to medium-high.
3. Drain cashews, rinse, dry and roast in pan until slightly brown.
4. Add a small amount of boxed bone broth to the pan to prevent ground beef from sticking.
5. Add ground beef and cook till brown.
6. At some point, the ground beef will give off a lot of water and steam. It's at this point you add 2 scoops (20 g) of collagen peptides.
7. Salt to taste.

MACRONUTRIENTS PER SERVING: CALORIES: 349 FAT: 21 G CARBS: 5 G PROTEIN: 37 G

MAKES 4 SERVINGS

COOKING TIME:
30 MINUTES

Sure, it's not 100% carnivore, but trust us, it's worth it.

PEANUT BUTTER STEAK SKEWERS

1 pound (454 g) sirloin steak

2 tablespoons (30 g) peanut butter

1 tablespoon (15 g) tomato paste

2 tablespoons (16 g) cayenne pepper

1 tablespoon (15 g) sea salt

1 medium (160 g) onion

4 skewer sticks

1. Preheat grill to medium-low.
2. Mix together tomato paste, peanut butter, and cayenne pepper in a big bowl.
3. Chop sirloin steak into skewer-sized cubes and season with sea salt.
4. Add steak to bowl, covering the pieces in the marinade.
5. Dip skewers in water to prevent burning on grill.
6. Peel and chop onion into quarters.
7. Add steak to skewers with an onion slice in between each piece of steak.
8. Grill on medium-low heat until meat is cooked to medium-well on the inside.
9. Let rest for 5-15 minutes before serving.

MACRONUTRIENTS PER SERVING: CALORIES: 289 FAT: 18 G CARBS: 5 G PROTEIN: 25 G

Trader Joe's Organic Valencia
Crunchy Salted Peanut Butter is
naturally sweet and rich. Enjoy

MAKES 4 SERVINGS

COOKING TIME:
20 MINUTES

POOR MAN'S *REVERSE SEAR* "RIBEYE"

A meat thermometer will make getting this recipe just right. Make sure you invest in one!

1 pound (454 g) beef chuck steak

1 tablespoon (15 g) beef tallow

Sea salt

1. Preheat oven to 225F (107C) or lowest possible temperature.
2. Season steak liberally with sea salt.
3. Cook in oven on an oven rack over a sheet pan.
4. Use a meat thermometer and cook until internal temperature reads 115-120F (46-49C).
5. Heat cast-iron or grill pan to high heat with a small bit of tallow.
6. When pan is smoking hot, sear steak for one minute or two per side.
7. Cut into thin slices and serve. No need to let rest.

MACRONUTRIENTS PER SERVING: CALORIES: 316 FAT: 24 G CARBS: 0 G PROTEIN: 22 G

MAKES 4 SERVINGS

COOKING TIME:
2 HOURS TO MARINATE
& 15 MINUTES
TO GRILL

Honey? Carnivore? Controversial, perhaps. Vegans reject honey as being an animal product, so we're embracing it as carnivores. Zero-carbers can feel free to skip or omit.

PORK SKEWERS

1 pound (454 g) lean pork

1 lime

¼ cup (60 ml) fish sauce

1 tablespoon (15 g) honey

1. Create marinade using fish sauce, honey, and juice of 1 lime.
2. Marinate for at least 2 hours, ideally for 4 hours, or overnight.
3. Soak skewers in cold water to prevent them from burning on the grill.
4. Heat up grill to medium-high.
5. Cut up pork into half-a-thumb-sized strips and thread on skewers.
6. Grill until golden and crispy on the outside.

MACRONUTRIENTS PER SERVING: CALORIES: 169 FAT: 4 G CARBS: 5 G PROTEIN: 28 G

MAKES 1 SERVING

PREP TIME:
5 MINUTES

RAW CARNIVORE CARPACCIO

Dip your toe in the truly savage world of eating raw meat. When eating raw meat, be extra sure to source from a high-quality, reputable source.

½ pound (228 g) top sirloin

Sea salt

1 ounce (28 g) shaved parmesan

1 ounce (28 g) anchovies

***Optional*: extra virgin olive or avocado oil**

1. Cut any fat off of beef and freeze for 30 minutes to 1 hour, so it's firm and very cold but not completely frozen.
2. Use a sharp knife to cut extremely thin pieces of meat.
3. Lay slices of meat on parchment or wax paper and pound flat with a mallet.
4. Serve on a cold plate (easiest to freeze plate at same time as meat).
5. Top with your fanciest sea salt, and garnish with shaved parmesan and sliced anchovies (and drizzle with optional extra virgin olive or avocado oil).

MACRONUTRIENTS PER SERVING: CALORIES: 282 FAT: 11 G CARBS: 0 G PROTEIN: 43 G

MAKES 2 SERVINGS

COOKING TIME:
15 MINUTES

SALT-TENDERIZED LONDON BROIL

A cool, minimalist way to tenderize otherwise tougher, less desirable cuts of meat.

2 6-ounce (170 g) top round steaks (London broil), about 2 inches thick

Sea salt

1 tablespoon (15 g) beef tallow

1. Cover each side of the steaks in a thick layer of sea salt. (For every inch of steak thickness wait 1 hour for salt to soak in.)
2. Rinse sea salt from steak and then season with an even layer of sea salt.
3. Melt beef tallow in a cast-iron pan on medium-high heat.
4. When grill is smoking hot, add steak to pan.
5. Cook for about 5 minutes, flip, and then cook for another 5 minutes on other side.
6. Let rest for 5 minutes before serving.

MACRONUTRIENTS PER SERVING: CALORIES: 332 FAT: 15 G CARBS: 0 G PROTEIN: 45 G

MAKES 1 SERVING

COOKING TIME:
45 MINUTES

Beef ain't the only red meat! Let's switch things up and try some of these delicious lamb chops.

SEARED LAMB CHOPS

4 ounces (113 g) lamb chops

1 dash sea salt

1 dash black pepper

1. Heat oven to 400F (204C). Pat chops dry with a paper towel, then season generously with sea salt and pepper.
2. Place in a frying pan and heat over medium-high heat until smoking. Add lamb chops and cook until golden-brown crust forms on the bottom, about 3 minutes. Flip and cook until the second side is golden brown-crusted, another 3 minutes.
3. Transfer lamb chops to baking tray and roast for 8-10 minutes. Remove from the oven and let rest for 5 minutes before serving.

MACRONUTRIENTS PER SERVING: CALORIES: 298 FAT: 23 G CARBS: 0 G PROTEIN: 27 G

MAKES 4 SERVINGS

COOKING TIME:
15 MINUTES

SIRLOIN STEAK BITES

When Brian lived in an apartment, he relied on a small yakatori-style electric grill to eat steak on a regular basis. Search amazon for simple electric grills for less than $50. The key to cooking steak on a small electric grill is to cook small pieces of meat rather than large steaks, which is why this recipe became a staple.

1 pound (454 g) top sirloin steak

Sea salt

1. Preheat electric grill to medium-high.
2. Slice sirloin steaks so they're about ½-inch thick.
3. Cut again into bite-sized, golf ball, or smaller-sized pieces.
4. Season with sea salt.
5. Add to grill, flipping and moving steak around the grill frequently to make sure all pieces are cooked evenly.
6. Serve medium-rare to medium-well with a big ramekin of your favorite dipping sauce. (I recommend Primal Kitchen Classic BBQ Sauce.)

MACRONUTRIENTS PER SERVING: CALORIES: 150 FAT: 4 G CARBS: 0 G PROTEIN: 26 G

MAKES 1 SERVING

PREP TIME:
20 MINUTES

STEAK TARTARE

Raw meat?! That's right, you savage. You got this. On the other hand, this is often seen as a hoity-toity delicacy. So, whether you're refined or a brute—enjoy some tartare!*

4 ounces (113 g) high-quality, fresh beef tenderloin

2 raw large egg yolks

Optional:

Sea salt

Black pepper

Mustard

Lemon juice

1. Place tenderloin in freezer for 15 minutes to slightly freeze, making it easier to slice.
2. Dice tenderloin into very thin slices. You can stack the thin slices and cut crosswise. Cut the beef as finely as possible, then dice it a few more times to fully mince it up.
3. Boom! Now plate and serve with your favorite garnishes. Some mustard is traditional. Salt to taste, add a little black pepper, and finally, two raw yolks on top! Some lemon juice also makes a nice touch.

****Note:***
Ensure raw food safety by talking with your butcher!

MACRONUTRIENTS PER SERVING: CALORIES: 301 FAT: 16 G CARBS: 0 G PROTEIN: 37 G

MAKES 2 SERVINGS

COOKING TIME: 3 HOURS

WALT'S MANLY ROAST

Walt Whitman was the original paleo health guru. His diet recommendation: a pound (454 g) of lean beef twice a day served with an optional stale piece of bread or boiled potato (skip that part). Be sure to have a meat thermometer for this one.

2 pounds (908 g) top round, bottom round, or eye of round beef roast

1 tablespoon (15 g) beef tallow

Sea salt

1. Cover meat with sea salt and bring to room temperature.
2. Preheat oven to 250F (121C) or lowest possible oven temperature.
3. Heat tallow in cast-iron pan on medium-high heat.
4. Sear until brown on all sides, about 3 minutes per side.
5. Transfer to oven and cook for 60-90 minutes. Use a meat thermometer and cook until internal temperature reaches 115F (46C).
6. Turn off oven and leave roast in oven for another 40 minutes, or until roast reaches internal temperature of 130F (54C) for medium-rare and 140F (60C) for medium.
7. Remove from oven and allow to rest for minutes.
8. Slice the meat to desired thickness. Eat half for breakfast/lunch and half for dinner.

MACRONUTRIENTS PER SERVING: CALORIES: 785 FAT: 43 G CARBS: 0 G PROTEIN: 100 G

OFFAL

MAKES 1 SERVING

COOKING TIME:
15 MINUTES

BACON AND LIVER!

You know damn well liver's good for you. And you could be experiencing the superhuman benefits of the carnivore diet if only you could stop gagging at the thought of liver. We gotchu. By quickly searing liver in bacon fat—you get all the delicious taste of bacon on the liver. You also avoid overcooking the liver, which leads to the gnarly, chalky taste and consistency people hate.

4 oz (113 g) calf liver

5 strips bacon

1. Set pan to medium heat. Add 5 strips bacon.
2. Let cook until bacon is firm. Flip occasionally to cook evenly.
3. Plate bacon and cover with paper towel.
4. Add liver to pan. Sear for 20 seconds on each side.
5. Enjoy!

MACRONUTRIENTS PER SERVING: CALORIES: 415 FAT: 25 G CARBS: 4 G PROTEIN: 45 G

MAKES 1 SERVING

COOKING TIME:
2 HOURS

BEST GRILLED LIVER

The combo of sesame oil and honey in this recipe is really outstanding. Give it a try and you'll see for yourself that liver is tastier than you ever imagined.

6 ounces (170 g) beef liver

1 cup (240 ml) whole milk

¼ cup (60 ml) fish sauce

Juice from ½ lemon

1 teaspoon (5 ml) sesame oil

1 teaspoon (5 g) honey

Optional: **1 teaspoon (5 g) MSG**

1. Soak liver in milk for about 1 hour.
2. Mix fish sauce, lemon juice, honey, and sesame oil in a bowl, and marinate liver in fridge for another hour or more.
3. Preheat grill and spray with cooking spray to prevent sticking.
4. When grill is hot, quickly sear 1-2 minutes per side, careful not to overcook the inside.

Optional:
Sprinkle MSG on liver as it's cooking.

MACRONUTRIENTS PER SERVING: CALORIES: 423 FAT: 14 G CARBS: 17 G PROTEIN: 57 G

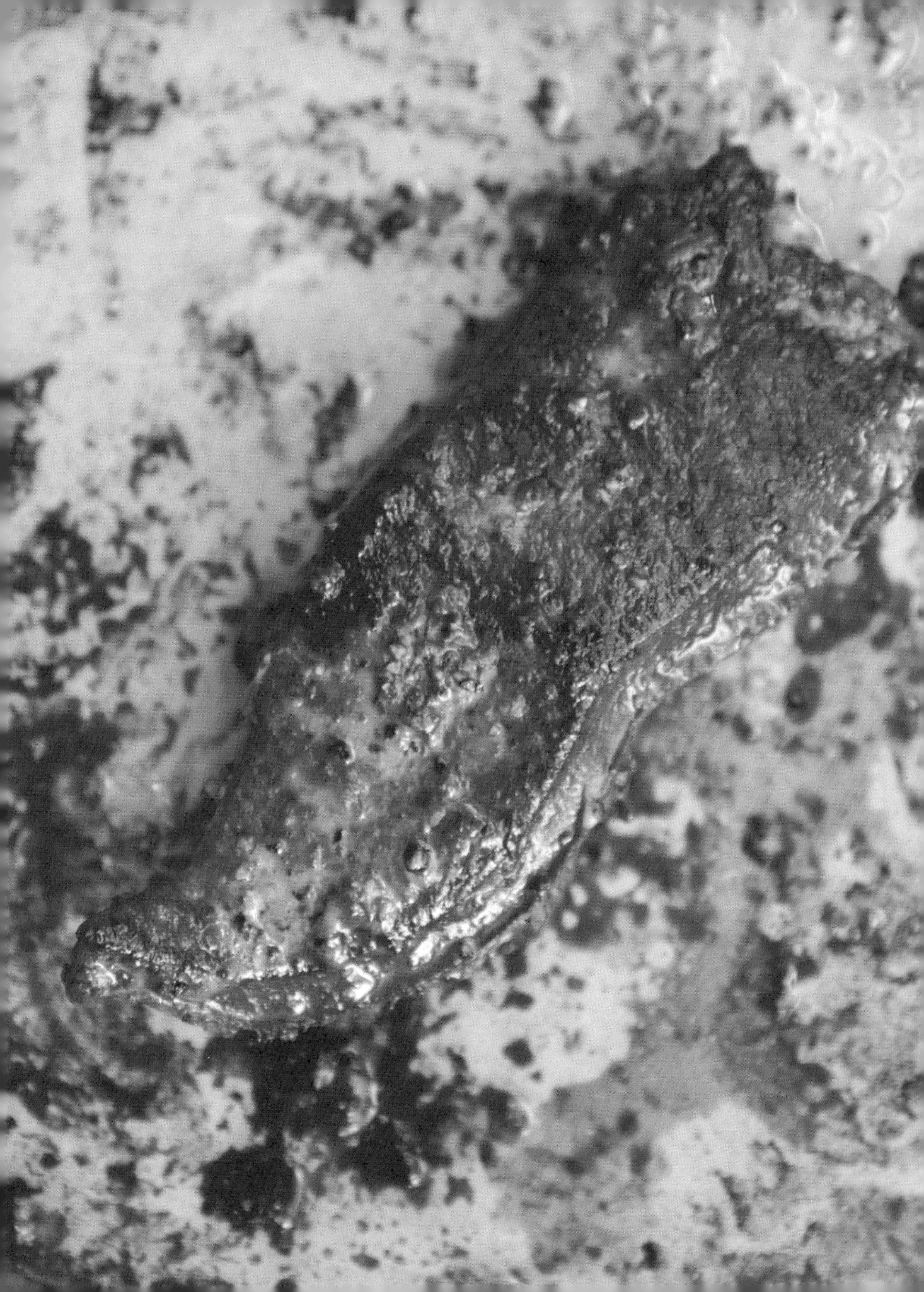

MAKES 8 CUPS

COOKING TIME:
5-8 HOURS

CARNIVORE
BONE BROTH

What could be more carnivore than making broth...from bones! You'll get the benefits of collagen, calcium, fatty acids, and vitamins A and K for reduced inflammation, healthy joints, and great skin.

Leftover bones with some meat on them

Himalayan pink salt

1. Fill up slow cooker with water.
2. Gather up leftover bones: T-bone, ribeye, short ribs, lamb bones, fish bones—all work fine! If there is some meat left on the bones, this will improve electrolyte content of your bone broth. Add these to the pot.
3. Add salt.
4. Set slow cooker to high and cook for 5-8 hours.
5. Remove bones and take meat off. Enjoy with pink salt!
6. Let bone broth cool before pouring into cup. Pour bone broth into cup and store the rest in mason jars.
7. Add a pinch of pink salt and serve!

MACRONUTRIENTS PER SERVING: CALORIES: 50 FAT: 3 G CARBS: 0 G PROTEIN: 2 G

MAKES 4 SERVINGS

COOKING TIME:
15 MINUTES

CHEESE CRISPS AND LIVER PÂTÉ

Cheese crisps are the ultimate carnivore hack if you need some crunch back in your life. Combine with liver pâté and you've got a formidable micronutrient punch!

1 tablespoon (15 g) butter

1 pound (454 g) beef liver

½ cup (120 ml) beef broth

1 bag of cheese crisps

Sea salt & pepper

1. Cut livers in half. Melt butter in pan on low heat. Add liver. Cook for 7-10 minutes, stirring occasionally.
2. Remove from heat and cool slightly. Add liver and broth to blender. Then puree with blender until smooth.
3. Add sea salt and pepper to taste. Pour pureed liver into glass dish or food container and refrigerate until chilled.
4. Serve with cheese crisps. Enjoy!

MACRONUTRIENTS PER SERVING: CALORIES: 194 FAT: 7 G CARBS: 4 G PROTEIN: 25 G

MAKES 1 SERVING

COOKING TIME:
15 MINUTES

CHICHARRONE NACHOS

An easy way to consume organ meats is to buy liverwurst or Braunschweiger from U.S. Wellness Meats and then use them in "junk-food" type recipes like this one.

1-ounce (28 g) bag of Epic Pork Rinds or 4505 Chicharrones

2 ounces (57 g) shredded cheese

4 ounces (113 g) U.S. Wellness Meats crumbled liverwurst or Braunschweiger

1 minced scallion

¼ cup minced fresh cilantro

1. Preheat oven to 450F (232C).
2. Add chicharrones to baking pan.
3. Top with 75% of the shredded cheese.
4. Add liverwurst or Braunschweiger.
5. Top with remaining 25% of cheese.
6. Bake for 5-10 minutes.
7. Remove pan from oven and add scallion and cilantro.

MACRONUTRIENTS PER SERVING: CALORIES: 654 FAT: 50 G CARBS –6 G PROTEIN: 46 G

POULTRY

MAKES 4 SERVINGS

COOKING TIME: 30 MINUTES

BACON-CRUSTED CHICKEN

Here's a delicious meal that will last you days! Dudes recommend Primal Kitchen Mayo—delicious stuff.

4 6-ounce (170 g) boneless and skinless chicken breasts

¼ cup (60 g) Primal Kitchen Mayo

1 ½ cups (340 g) bacon bits

¼ teaspoon (1.25 g) Himalayan pink salt

1. Preheat the oven to 450F (232C). Line a baking sheet with foil and grease lightly.
2. In a blender, blend the bacon bits and sea salt until there are tiny pieces left. Blend for 20-45 seconds. Add to a small bowl.
3. Coat each chicken breast with a thin layer of mayo, then sprinkle on the bacon mixture. Place on the baking sheet.
4. Bake for 15-20 minutes, until the chicken is fully cooked.

MACRONUTRIENTS PER SERVING: CALORIES: 347 FAT: 23 G CARBS: 0 G PROTEIN: 39 G

FRIED PORK

MAKES 4 SERVINGS

COOKING TIME:
15 MINUTES

CHICHARRONES CHICKEN STRIPS

Chicharrones are pork rinds, and we're doing backflips about how easy it is to use them to coat chicken breast in this recipe. Using bland flour seems like such a letdown after you try this brilliant idea.

1 2.5-ounce (60 g) bag Epic Pork Rinds or 4505 Chicharrones

1 pound (454 g) boneless and skinless chicken breast

2 large eggs

2 tablespoons (30 g) beef tallow

1. Cut chicken breast into thin strips.
2. Let the air out of the bag of chicharrones and crush into fine powder.
3. Crack eggs in a bowl and whisk. Then dip chicken strips in the egg mixture and coat in the chicharrons powder.
4. Melt beef tallow in a pan on medium-high heat.
5. Fry each battered strip for 4-5 minutes per side or until brown and crispy on all sides. (Option: These could also be cooked using an Air Fryer.)
6. Let rest and cool on a plate with paper towel before serving.

MACRONUTRIENTS PER SERVING: CALORIES: 336 FAT: 19 G CARBS: 0 G PROTEIN: 39 G

MAKES 4 SERVINGS

COOKING TIME:
20 MINUTES

CHICKEN-BACON-BEEF MUSCLE BOWL

Here's another Shewfelt classic. This type of simple and easy meal characterizes his carnivore diet. It's inexpensive, keeps your protein high, doesn't go overboard on the fat, and is delicious.

3 sliced chicken sausages

1 pound (454 g) ground beef

5 slices bacon

4 tablespoons (60 g) Primal Kitchen Spicy Ketchup

Sea salt

1. Set a large pan to medium heat. Add 5 slices of bacon to pan. Cook for 6-8 minutes.
2. Reduce heat to medium-low. Add sliced chicken sausage and 1 pound (454 g) of ground beef. Mix together. Cook for 5-8 minutes.
3. Remove from heat and strain off excess fat before serving. Serve with Primal Kitchen Spicy Ketchup and salt to taste.

MACRONUTRIENTS PER SERVING: CALORIES: 360 FAT: 23 G CARBS: 4 G PROTEIN: 34 G

MAKES 4 SERVINGS

COOKING TIME:
15 MINUTES

CHICKEN HEART SKEWERS

These skewers are a Mediterranean classic. All of the amazing nutrients of chicken hearts with a nice kick from cumin.

1 pound (454 g) chicken hearts (thawed)

Sea salt

Pepper

Cayenne

Cumin

1. Heat grill to medium-high heat. Load up each skewer with 5-6 thawed chicken hearts.
2. Season generously with sea salt, pepper, cayenne, and some cumin as desired.
3. Set on grill and cook until firm throughout. Enjoy!

MACRONUTRIENTS PER SERVING: CALORIES: 176 FAT: 11 G CARBS: 1 G PROTEIN: 18 G

MAKES 2 SERVINGS

COOKING TIME:
20 MINUTES

Add some excitement to the boring, but macro-friendly, boneless, skinless chicken breasts. We also recommend eating these with Primal Kitchen BBQ sauces or mixing Primal Kitchen Mustard with Primal Kitchen Mayo to make a dipping sauce.

CRUNCHY CHICKEN STICKS WITH DIPPING SAUCE

2 4-ounce boneless and skinless chicken breasts

3 raw large egg yolks

1 tablespoon (15 g) yellow mustard

Sea salt

***Optional:* pickles**

1. Preheat grill to medium heat.
2. Cut chicken breasts lengthwise into strips about an inch in diameter.
3. Spray grill to avoid sticking.
4. Add chicken strips to hot grill on elevated rack and cover.
5. Turn every few minutes.
6. Mix 3 egg yolks with 1 tablespoon (15 g) mustard in a ramekin (this is your dipping sauce).
7. Grill chicken strips until brown and crispy on the outside (what most would consider overcooked). They should have the firmness of a restaurant chicken strip.
8. Serve with dipping sauce and a side of pickles.

MACRONUTRIENTS PER SERVING: CALORIES: 197 FAT: 10 G CARBS: 1 G PROTEIN: 26 G

MAKES 8 SERVINGS

COOKING TIME:
1 HOUR
AND 40 MINUTES

EASY ROAST CHICKEN

Roasting a whole, organic chicken is a simple, easy, and cost-effective option on a carnivore diet.

1 3.5-pound (1589 g) whole organic chicken

1 tablespoon (15 g) Himalayan pink salt

1 tablespoon (15 g) dried poultry herbs

Black pepper

1. Preheat oven to 350F (177C).
2. Remove room temperature chicken from packaging and rinse.
3. Place chicken on baking pan and stuff cavity with herbs and black pepper.
4. Rub in the rest of the herbs and all of the salt on the outside of the chicken.
5. Bake for 90 minutes.
6. Place the chicken on a platter and drizzle the fat from the baking pan over its top.
7. Enjoy!

MACRONUTRIENTS PER SERVING: CALORIES: 315 FAT: 20 G CARBS: 1 G PROTEIN: 35 G

MAKES 4 SERVINGS

COOKING TIME:
30 MINUTES

FISH SAUCE
CHICKEN WINGS

These wings are perfect to grill up for your next party. They're packed with flavor and won't put you in a food coma only to miss out on the actual party.

¼ cup (60 ml) fish sauce

¼ cup (60 g) honey

4 minced garlic cloves

Juice from 3 fresh limes

1 pound (454 g) bone-in chicken wings

1 teaspoon (5 g) red pepper flakes

1. In a bowl, mix fish sauce, honey, lime juice, and minced garlic to make marinade.
2. Marinate wings for 3-4 hours or overnight.
3. Preheat grill and spray with cooking oil to prevent sticking.
4. Cook on medium-low on elevated rack.
5. Before wings are completely done cooking, toss in marinade a second time, season with red pepper flakes, and then quickly sear on lower part of the grill.

MACRONUTRIENTS PER SERVING: CALORIES: 260 FAT: 15 G CARBS: 8 G PROTEIN: 25 G

MAKES 2 SERVINGS

COOKING TIME:
1 HOUR

Try this bodybuilder classic! You might not look like Arnold, but this meal will definitely terminate that belly fat and turn you from a girly man into Conan the Carnivore. This makes for a delicious meal with minimal prep time—seriously, it doesn't get any easier than this, guys.

GRILLED CHICKEN AND COTTAGE CHEESE

1 pound (454 g) boneless and skinless chicken breasts

Himalayan pink salt

Black pepper

1 tablespoon (15 g) grass-fed butter

1 ½ cups (122 g) organic full-fat cottage cheese

1. Preheat oven to 375F (177C).
2. Melt butter in pan, then coat each breast lightly in butter. Season with pink salt and a dash of black pepper.
3. Place chicken in glass baking dish. Bake uncovered in oven for 45 minutes, until chicken is golden brown and the juices run clear.
4. Plate chicken and add ¾ cup (122 g) of cottage cheese on the side of each breast. Enjoy!

MACRONUTRIENTS PER SERVING: CALORIES: 503 FAT: 19 G CARBS: 6 G PROTEIN: 72 G

MAKES 4 SERVINGS

COOKING TIME:
30 MINUTES

HOT SAUCE CHICKEN WINGS

Everyone loves some chicken wings! This spicy dish is perfect for game day.

1 pound (454 g) bone-in chicken wings

1 tablespoon (15 ml) olive oil

1 teaspoon (5 g) garlic powder

Sea salt

Black pepper

2 tablespoons (30 g) sour cream

Tabasco sauce

1. Set oven to 480F (249C).
2. Coat the wings with olive oil and garlic powder.
3. Season well with sea salt and pepper.
4. Place the wings on baking sheet and bake in oven for 20 minutes.
5. Serve with sour cream dip and Tabasco sauce!

MACRONUTRIENTS PER SERVING: CALORIES: 294 FAT: 23 G CARBS: 1 G PROTEIN: 21 G

MAKES 8 SERVINGS

COOKING TIME:
1 HOUR
AND 15 MINUTES

Be warned—tomatoes will be involved! If you are on a strict carnivore diet—than leave out the tomatoes! They're simply for flavor.

INDIAN BUTTER CHICKEN

2 pounds (908 g) boneless and skinless chicken thighs, cut in pieces

1 28-ounce (794 g) can of tomatoes, crushed, pureed, sauce, or marinara

1 cup (240 g) full-fat sour cream

Curry powder to taste

Sea salt

1 tablespoon (15 g) butter

1. Preheat oven to 300F (149C).
2. Heat cast-iron Dutch oven over medium-high heat. Add butter to coat bottom of pot.
3. Sear chicken for 3-4 minutes on each side
4. Add tomatoes and deglaze pot. Add curry powder and stir well.
5. Cover in oven for 1 hour. Stir in sour cream before serving. Salt to taste.
6. Enjoy!

MACRONUTRIENTS PER SERVING: CALORIES: 266 FAT: 12 G CARBS: 11 G PROTEIN: 27 G

MAKES 8 SERVINGS

COOKING TIME:
40 MINUTES

These lemon pepper chicken thighs are incredible to mix things up with your usual fare of steak, eggs, and fish. Give this a shot!

LEMON PEPPER CHICKEN THIGHS

2 pounds (908 g) bone-in chicken thighs

5 tablespoons (75 g) butter

2 tablespoons (30 ml) lemon juice

Lemon pepper

Himalayan pink salt

1. Preheat oven to 400F (204C).
2. Season chicken thighs with pink salt and lemon pepper.
3. Heat 2 tablespoons (30 g) butter in oven-proof skillet over medium heat. Add chicken and cook for 5-6 minutes until crispy.
4. Flip chicken thighs over and transfer skillet to oven. Bake for 15-20 minutes.
5. Transfer skillet back to stove. Plate chicken. Add remaining butter and lemon juice to pan on medium-high heat and mix into sauce.
6. Pour sauce over top of chicken.

MACRONUTRIENTS PER SERVING: CALORIES: 191 FAT: 17 G CARBS: 0 G PROTEIN: 11 G

MAKES 2 SERVINGS

TOTAL TIME:
5 MINUTES

POOR MAN'S
TERIYAKI CHICKEN

We're calling this "poor man's," but it's actually pretty high-end because it's flavored with superior ingredients such as fish sauce and coconut aminos and amped up with collagen.

2 12.5-ounce (354 g) cans of Kirkland canned chicken breast

2 tablespoons (30 ml) Red Boat Fish Sauce

1 tablespoon (15 g) honey

1 tablespoon (9 g) unflavored hydrolyzed collagen

⅓ cup (90 ml) chicken bone broth

***Optional:* 2 tablespoons (30 ml) coconut aminos**

***Optional:* 2 tablespoons (30 ml) sesame oil**

1. Add gelatin and bone broth to a bowl.
2. Open can of chicken, drain, and add to bowl.
3. Add fish sauce and honey.
4. Mix thoroughly with fork.
5. Add in coconut aminos for even more of a "soy sauce" like flavor and a few drops of sesame oil for a real Asian-inspired kick.

MACRONUTRIENTS PER SERVING: CALORIES: 427 FAT: 6 G CARBS: 9 G PROTEIN: 87 G

MAKES 4 SERVINGS

COOKING TIME:
40 MINUTES

This delicious chicken dish has a spicy kick to it. Easy to make and pretty fast!

SMOKED PAPRIKA CHICKEN

1 tablespoon (15 g) butter

1 tablespoon (15 ml) olive oil

1 tablespoon (7 g) smoked paprika

Garlic pepper salt

¼ cup (15 g) parsley

1 pound (454 g) boneless and skinless chicken breast

1. In a small bowl, combine 1 tablespoon (15 ml) olive oil, smoked paprika, garlic pepper salt, and parsley to create a smooth paste. Massage paste into chicken breasts. Let stand for at least 20 minutes to allow the meat to absorb the flavor.

2. Set the oven to broil and place a rack in the upper third of the oven. Place chicken breasts on a foil-lined baking sheet. Place chicken under the broiler for 7-8 minutes or until a crust begins to form around the edges.

3. Flip the breasts and cook them under the broiler for another 7 to 8 minutes or until cooked throughout. Cooking time may depend on your oven's heat. Most important is to make sure chicken breasts are cooked throughout.

4. Once cooked, let the breasts rest for a minute or two before serving to allow the juices to evenly distribute through the meat. Sprinkle with chopped parsley and serve!

MACRONUTRIENTS PER SERVING: CALORIES: 167 FAT: 9 G CARBS: 0 G PROTEIN: 22 G

INDEX

D

E

F

G

H

I

K

L

M

R

S

T

U

V

W

Y